A CLERGY H
SURVIVAL GUIDE

Matthew Caminer

First published in Great Britain in 2012

Society for Promoting Christian Knowledge
36 Causton Street
London SW1P 4ST
www.spckpublishing.co.uk

British Library Cataloguing-in-Publication Data
A catalogue record for this book is available from the British Library

ISBN 978–0–281–06790–9
eBook ISBN 978–0–281–06791–6

Typeset by Graphicraft Limited, Hong Kong
First printed in Great Britain by Ashford Colour Press
Subsequently digitally printed in Great Britain

To Miriam
without whose ordination
this book would not have been written
and to
clergy husbands everywhere

About the author

———•·•◆•·•———

Matthew Caminer is a management consultant specializing in process improvement. His career has involved him in projects across industry, the public sector and the Church, including membership of a Consultants to Teams pilot group for the churches in Scotland and consultancy projects for the dioceses of Glasgow and Oxford. Matthew has had a number of leadership roles in the Cursillo movement, and is currently a member of the Making Disciples Strategy Development Group for the Diocese of Oxford. He met his wife Miriam, who was ordained in 2011, when they were both soloists in a performance of Handel's *Messiah*. *A Clergy Husband's Survival Guide* is Matthew's first book.

Contents

————◆◆◆————

Contents

Part 4
IF THINGS GO WRONG

Introduction

One Sunday afternoon a few weeks after Miriam's ordination, the doorbell rang. We were lounging in the living room with our feet up, watching an old film on TV amid the weekend papers and the wreckage of lunch. Answering the summons, I found a member of the congregation standing on the doorstep. 'It's your wife I need,' he said, holding a document that required her signature. It was a perfectly pleasant interlude, lasting only a few minutes, but it wryly underlined Miriam's role as curate and mine, in this instance, as mere door opener. In all sorts of ways, life was changing.

Ordination involves a major shift. You can't be 'half ordained'. Before her ordination, Miriam wasn't, and now she is. When we were out and about in those first weeks after Miriam began wearing her collar, whether in parks, restaurants or shops, she would find herself engaged in conversation by total strangers, given a sideways look, or simply treated differently from before. I, in the meantime, hitherto the upfront and outgoing one, would be totally ignored. Miriam's new public persona was not something we had discussed in much depth. In fact it was only now dawning on us – and especially on me – that virtually every aspect of our way of life, the things we had taken for granted throughout our marriage, and our relationships with others, were about to change for ever, however positively.

In some ways, you might have expected us to be prepared for all this. Miriam had been a Reader for 17 years, and her work as a spiritual director meant people regularly came to see her in our home. On those occasions, I had to make myself scarce, and although I developed a friendly, neutral telephone manner, I rarely met any of those she directed. In any case, at that time my business life took me out on the road for days or weeks at a time, so Miriam's work didn't impinge very much. More recently, though, I have taken on a new existence as a self-employed management consultant, and the periods between contracts are becoming longer, with retirement on the horizon. Thus the impact of Miriam's new role on the household, and on our life, is becoming greater at a time when I am already going through a lot of changes of my own.

Talking to other clergy husbands, I soon discovered that their perspectives varied widely. Some expressed the belief that they shared a joint ministry with their wives: some were even ordained themselves. Conversely, there were those who felt so separated from their wife's ministry that they refused to answer questions because, as far they were concerned, it simply didn't affect them and, honestly, they wished it wasn't happening at all. I stand somewhere in the middle. I certainly support Miriam's journey with joy and enthusiasm; I am a sounding board and, if invited, I give advice. But I do not believe that this is a joint ministry. It is her vocation.

Miriam's journey towards ordination was a slow burn lasting many years. Throughout this time, and as the pace picked up, I remained a benign spectator with little sense of needing to prepare for the life of a clergy husband. I was formally involved in the process only twice: after all, it was Miriam's vocation and suitability for ordination that were being scrutinized, not mine. The machinery which was carrying her towards the finishing line did nothing to move me forward. The potential impact on our lives was not ignored: it simply didn't occur to us to explore it.

The staff at the theological college did their best to be warm, welcoming and inclusive. There was a chaplain to the spouses, and at the beginning of the process I met Miriam's head of studies. I went to an introductory evening and spouses were invited to sit in on lectures as often as we liked, but I felt that I should give Miriam the space to get fully involved without any distractions. In any case, her Tuesday evenings and occasional weekends at college represented quality undiluted 'me time'!

I gradually became conscious of the need to find out a bit more about life as a clergy husband. I looked for help, but couldn't find any accessible resources or up to date material. Books, reflections, anthologies and web sites seemed to come and go. Of these, some were couched in the language of psychology or densely packed theology, neither of which felt practical or accessible: too many words, not enough pointers. Others felt like rather self-congratulatory reflections on life as a clergy wife (and yes, I do mean clergy wife. I still had not found anything relating to real experience as a clergy husband). I knew that I needed to explore, but not knowing what I didn't know, had no idea where to start.

Gradually, however, three things became clear: (a) that everyone is different, as are their situations and needs, so a 'one size fits all' response was not going to be of much help; (b) that appropriate resources, whether printed, on line, or in the form of a support group (especially one proactively supported by the diocese or theological college) would be of value; and (c) that my desire for help was clearly shared by others in the same situation in life.

Being a bit of a pragmatist, the answer was obvious: fill the gap myself. This book is the result.

Although Miriam's journey has provided me with a certain amount of experience, it represents only a single perspective. It certainly could not provide the objectivity required to address all the issues that were now bubbling to the surface. You will therefore see references to research that I undertook during 2011. This was based on an electronic survey for which the contributors, nearly all clergy husbands, answered a series of open-ended questions. They were encouraged to respond in as much depth as possible, sharing feelings, both positive and negative, and giving examples. There were 48 responses from 14 Anglican dioceses in the United Kingdom and Europe. The respondents were admittedly self-selecting and the research is unscientific in purely statistical terms. Despite these short-comings, it has provided a rich source of material based on authentic situations in a wide variety of contexts. Throughout the book, I have quoted directly from contributors' responses; to differentiate these quotations from others, they are printed thus:

I try to prepare for the unexpected and never forget that God is in this with me.

A number of the contributors asked not to be identified in the book. In the interest of consistency, therefore, none of the quotations are attributed by name or location. The willingness of the clergy husbands concerned to contribute is warmly acknowledged.

You may wonder why this book is about clergy husbands and not about clergy spouses in general. The approach arises in part because the concept of a clergy husband is relatively new and very little has been written about it. But even a cursory analysis of Church of England statistics for new ordinations demonstrates that the mix of male v. female and stipendiary v. self-supporting clergy shows interesting contrasts, and the profile has continued to evolve since the first ordination of women to the priesthood in 1994. There has been a steady rise in the proportion of female ordinations, to the point that by 2010 there was almost a 50:50 mix. Furthermore, whereas only one in three new male clergy are self-supporting (previously known as non-stipendiary), nearly two-thirds of women are. These are only two of a number of factors that point to significant difference. It is of course dangerous to generalize, but as a working hypothesis, there is a good case for this focus on clergy husbands. This discussion is developed in Chapter 8.

This book is in four parts, which you are invited to read through from start to finish, or which you may prefer to dip into.

Part One looks at the journey from the emergence of an idea that there may be a vocation, to training, ordination and the early days of the first curacy. It touches also on the occasions when, as the husband, you may expect to be involved formally. Part Two considers what it is to be a clergy husband and the need to know yourself, as we look at areas of opinion and perspective. It shows that there are widely differing points of view on the matter, and that as a clergy husband, you have to develop your own understanding and approach. Part Three explores some of the practical themes of day-to-day life, organization of the home and time management, and the issues that may affect your quality of life as the husband and family of female clergy.

Sadly, things may go wrong and Part Four highlights some potentially problematic areas. They may not apply to you now and, all being well, they will never do so. Ideally, an understanding of the factors discussed in the first three parts will help to prevent at least some of these hazards from developing into cataclysms that threaten your marriage, career or health.

Throughout these four parts, there are questions, suggestions and things to think through by yourself or in discussion with your wife, with others in the same boat or with a trusted friend. This book is not just for clergy husbands, but is also addressed to your ordained wives, to those in your immediate circle and to those looking in on your situation from the outside, especially those providing support or oversight. They may use the same questions to underline the wide range of needs that exist among clergy husbands and to review approaches to communication, training and support.

A recurring theme is the need to develop a circle of trusted friends because it is so easy to feel isolated when difficulties arise. While this book may be helpful in developing an understanding of the life of a clergy husband, therefore, it should emphatically not be seen as a self-help manual to be used at a time of crisis: that is when those trusted friends may represent critical sources of support and rescue.

You may already have formed the view that my emphasis is a little jaundiced, when the life of faith is one to be celebrated with joy and optimism. My intention, though, is that by taking what may at times seem a slightly pessimistic approach, you may come out at the other end with greater clarity and optimism.

I hope that as fellow clergy husbands, and especially those just starting out, you will find that *A Clergy Husband's Survival Guide* helps to clear the path and provides practical signposts for the journey.

Part 1

THE JOURNEY

'Darling . . . I think I'm meant to be a priest.'

Whether or not that message is a surprise, and whether or not it is welcome, from the moment you hear it your marriage will never be the same again. Even if the idea is tested and doesn't lead anywhere, your wife will have gone through a time of change and so will you. For the purposes of this book, however, let's assume that she goes ahead and travels the full journey: what does that journey look like, how might you get involved, and what impact will it have on you?

As soon as your wife raises the idea of offering herself for ordination, you will be a fellow traveller, regardless of whether you are fully involved or simply a spectator. More than that, it will affect your life, your marriage, your family and your relationships. In this part of the book, we take a husband's-eye view of the journey, looking at the areas in which you may be involved directly or indirectly. Along the way we will explore the following themes:

- It's a very long process.

- You are part of the journey.

- Some of what happens will baffle you!

- You will probably be interviewed for your wife's job.

- Been divorced? Or your wife? Prepare yourself: it won't be pretty!

- Know where to find help.

- Communication is essential.

This book is mainly for and about the husbands of female clergy who have already started their life of ministry. If, however, your wife is at a much earlier stage, or indeed is still exploring, then this brief walk through the complete journey is also for you. It doesn't pretend to be an authoritative guide to 'How do I get ordained?' That is the job of the church authorities, especially as there may be local variations. What it does offer, however, is an exploration of the potential impact on you and your wife, especially at those times when you are likely to be directly involved.

1

The process

... is not by any to be enterprised, nor taken in hand, unadvisedly, lightly, or wantonly ...   (Book of Common Prayer)

I don't see it as any different to being the husband of a business woman apart from the hours being different.

The process that culminates in ordination is a long one, and deliberately so. Your wife will have to meet a lot of different people before she faces the ordeal of the Bishops' Advisory Panel, or BAP. It takes a long time because the vocation must be tested for its authenticity, something you may well understand intellectually without necessarily appreciating the full implications. However positive both you and your wife may feel, the process will certainly involve adopting a different way of life based on fresh assumptions. The lengthy and often disruptive period of training and formation that follows a successful outcome from the BAP is equally likely to affect your family life, involving your home, your lifestyle and your finances, and possibly requiring you to move house or change jobs.

Let's now look at the stages that are involved and their potential impact on you. Not everyone will go through the same steps in the same sequence. The stages will differ from diocese to diocese and to an extent will depend on the amount of experience your wife has had before entering the journey. It is similarly difficult to generalize about how long it will all take and how many meetings there will be: these are subject to many factors, some with local variations that need to be understood.

Personal reflection

You may be part of this process. It may even be you who suggests to your wife that she should explore her vocation. This is a time of evolution, in which the spark of that vocation will be explored and tested, perhaps for months or years, before it becomes appropriate to develop the search into a more formal dialogue. It is an exciting time, but it may also be unsettling.

Discussion/s with incumbent

It's unlikely that your wife will be able to make any practical steps towards ordination without the support of her incumbent. This may even mean moving churches to find someone to provide that support, something which may affect you in all sorts of ways. If doors appear to slam shut, you are likely to be the person who has to provide comfort in the face of distress, denial or anger. It will be even harder to offer that comfort if you share your wife's reactions.

Discussion/s with vocations advisor

The diocese will appoint a local vocations advisor whose job is to focus on your wife and her vocation. The impact on you and your family life will be secondary, if it is considered at all. Even at this early stage, however, you will need to explore the many ways in which your wife's eventual ordination will intrude on your marriage and family life. You may have to be proactive in starting this dialogue with your wife and the vocations advisor.

Discussion/s with Diocesan Director of Ordinands (DDO)

By now your wife's potential vocation will be gathering recognition, but there's a long way to go. The DDO will need to form his or her own view based on your wife's vocation and the needs of the diocese – not on you! Your wife may have a very clear calling to serve the Church in some capacity; indeed she may already be doing so. It is valid, though, for the Church to explore whether that vocation is for ordained ministry. The Church may not have a need for the particular shade of vocation, however godly, that your wife offers; even if it does, the diocese may not be able to afford it. You may both end up feeling baffled, distressed and angered at challenges that are raised, and you may be as bruised by the process as your wife, even if the eventual outcome is positive.

Discussion/s with bishop

The DDO has pushed your wife's case forward to the bishop: support for her vocation is clearly growing. The bishop must nevertheless form his own view, governed by a variety of factors. The needs of the diocese will again be on his mind, and he will be influenced by the body of paperwork that has by now accumulated in support of your wife's candidature. In the space of a single interview, to which you will probably not be invited, he has a decision to make. You, your family and your home circumstances are unlikely to be high on his agenda, however much you feel that this ought to be the case.

Bishops' Advisory Panel

Into the crucible! Three days of intensive grilling against nine fixed criteria. Your wife will have papers to submit in advance, and she will go through a series of gruelling interviews and other activities. She is being assessed against her vocation and her qualities. Your marriage and the impact on you and your home life are ruled out of scope: you are again not invited. The outcome may be a recommendation that your wife should be encouraged to go forward for training. Sometimes this comes with conditions, such as the suggestion that she should return after a suitable period during which she is to gain extra experience. In other cases, the verdict may be completely negative. There is no perfect way of passing on this sort of message. It is very often seen by the candidate as failure or rejection, and the Church is not always able to provide full support in the months that follow. This can lead to bitterness, anger, deep sadness and many other emotions for you both.

Training and formation

The training is likely to take three years and may be residential. It could mean moving house, finding a budget for books, perhaps a new computer. You may end up adding housework, cooking and child care to your day job. Indeed you may need to change your job altogether or alternatively live a parallel life, staying at home while she is away at theological college. How this will work out varies hugely between different dioceses and colleges. Similarly, the extent to which previous experience and formal academic qualifications are allowed to influence the content and duration of the training will vary widely. In some cases, the college will proactively seek to involve you, in others it may be a more half-hearted invitation, while in yet others you will not be considered at all. In summary, it may affect you almost as much as it affects your wife; do seek the opportunity for a thorough review of the options and potential consequences.

Ordination

This is a time to celebrate. Take the opportunity to rejoice and enjoy the moment, because your life as a clergy husband has just begun! For some, however, there may be uncertainty even at this stage, as ordination may take place before your wife's first parish has been finalized. For many people, ordination will coincide with moving house, in itself a highly stressful process. Even if your wife is going to exercise her ministry in the parish where you already live and worship, ordination is still a rite of passage, a doorway into a new way of life. To a certain extent, you too are going through that doorway. If you have had to change jobs in order to move with your wife to her new parish, then add yet another stress factor to the list!

Further training during curacy

Initial Ministerial Education (IME) entails a minimum of three years on-the-job study and building of experience. Whatever its form, and however long the training takes, it will affect you too. Few people realize in advance quite how onerous this training will be. Perhaps the biggest challenge is not for those in full-time ministry, but for those already in full- or part-time employment, perhaps with the extra burdens of child care, or care of other dependents. It is hard to imagine your wife settling into the new routine and the requirements of IME without you having to take on some additional responsibilities.

This lengthy gestation period is complicated further if either you or your wife, or both, have previously been divorced, since a faculty must be obtained. This adds a further dimension, and is an area that we explore in Chapter 3.

Some people argue that the lengthy training clergy undergo before they are let loose on congregations, and the continuing education they undertake following ordination, is no different from those required in some other professions. Medicine and the law, for instance, are known for their extensive training over many years. But there the similarity ceases. In Chapter 7 we contrast with other professions many of the characteristics of the life of ordained ministry.

Despite the appearance I may have given that the process of ordination entails a smooth sequence of events, the reality is that there are several opportunities for go/no-go decisions, whether made by your wife and yourself, or by those accompanying her on the journey of discernment. This may mean walking away from a life of ordained ministry altogether, or the suggestion that the vocation should be channelled in a different direction. It can be a time of huge strain and distress, not only for your wife but for you too. It is very much up to your dynamics as a couple how this works out.

From vocation to ordination: things you can do

- Listen to your wife. She will probably want to share on a number of levels, spiritual, emotional and practical.

- If you find it difficult to take seriously the prospect of your wife's ordination, or if you simply don't 'get it', find someone else to discuss it with. She may have been brewing the idea for years, and you need time to catch up.

- Encourage your wife to build up her own network of trusted friends. You may be too close to be objective and disinterested.

- Make sure you discuss and understand all the options for training (residential or non-residential, full time or part time) and type of ministry (stipendiary or self-supporting, full time or part time) and their implications. These choices will have a huge impact on your life and your career, not just your wife's.

- As your wife becomes more and more involved in the process, be proactive in protecting 'us' time and book leisure time in both your diaries. Go out on dates together and make sure you don't neglect the basic things in life.

- If you have children, or plan to have them, start thinking about the impact of your wife's journey on child care, schools and related matters, and plan ahead.

- As ordination approaches, consider how you may help to make life easier for your wife, whether in major areas where you can make a difference, or in special gestures. For instance, unless she wants to do it herself, take responsibility for organizing the party she will probably want to have afterwards.

- If you are a person of little or no faith or are of a different faith altogether, it is just as important, if not more so, for you to be aware of the impact of all that is going on around you and how you react. Share your feelings with someone you trust.

- Be aware that your wife will change and that so, possibly, may you. Celebrate the changes, but remind yourself and each other that there is a risk of marginalizing core characteristics of your relationship that need to be protected.

- Be aware of the post-ordination training needs. They often come as a surprise, and they will certainly affect you because of the huge drain they make on time, finances and energy. Insist on being involved in the discussion.

2

Meeting the DDO

For many clergy husbands, there will be a single occasion when you are formally involved in the process that your wife is going through. This is when there is a meeting, usually in your own home, with the vocations advisor or the DDO. Depending on the diocese, you will generally be invited to attend; you may even be expected to be present. The purpose of the meeting, you may assume, is to establish whether the marriage is secure, whether the wife's vocation and intention to enter a life of ministry has the committed support of the family. In one husband's experience, though:

> Call me cynical, but it seemed to me that it was as likely that all they really wanted to do was cover their backs and make sure there wasn't a risk that I would bring scandal on the church.

I know that my reaction, as the visit became closer, was to wonder why I was being interviewed for my wife's job. After all, even in the old days of the Diplomatic Corps, the wife (and it usually was the wife) was only wheeled in before an appointment was made in order to ensure that she conveyed the right social fit and wouldn't cause embarrassment. In those days an application might indeed potentially have been rejected on the grounds of 'Wife Impossible'.

Times and attitudes have changed. In any case, it could be argued that the establishment, whether embodied in the Church or another institution, has not yet developed expectations of the husbands of female candidates. Whereas there may be a stereotypical perception, however inappropriate, of what a 'vicar's wife' is like, the only pattern that has emerged for a clergy husband is that there is no pattern. This begs the question of what it is that the Church is looking for when the vocations advisor or the DDO invades the privacy of your home for a meeting with you.

It is hard to be prescriptive, because there does not appear to be a standard approach across the Church, as reported by clergy husbands from four dioceses:

Diocese A – Meeting at home: husband must be present.
Diocese B – Meeting at home: husband's presence optional.
Diocese C – Husband required to write a letter of commitment.
Diocese D – Husband's point of view not canvassed.

Let's look at the home visit from the point of view of a DDO in one diocese:

The purpose of the visit and what I intend to do is:

1 Get to know the spouse – if they are happy being known – so they know my face and I know theirs. Plus if things get stopped or go wrong it is better that the spouse can be invited and worked with as well – if candidate and spouse want that.
2 Given the strangeness of the process, I explain it to the spouse and candidate together – the candidate knows it but it relieves them from having to explain what may seem strange to them too.
3 Try and gauge the reaction of the spouse so this can honestly and openly be worked at. This is especially true where a faculty is required [see Chapter 3] and the spouse is involved in that regardless.

I try to ensure the candidate has explained it to the spouse – if the message hasn't got back I wonder about communication. I always explain anyway.

Personally some spouses (more often men) do not wish to be met with and are very suspicious of the situation. I try and work with the candidate to find out what this is about. If there is great antagonism, this is reported in the sponsorship papers with the candidate's full knowledge. This has been rare over my decade in the job. Generally people are curious, quite interested in this DDO person who they have heard of. I try to keep things relaxed and informal while giving as much help as I can, and learning as much as I can about how the marriage operates.

The feel of any meeting may be in part gender related (the more difficult ones have generally been with men, but then some of the most helpful ones have been with men too – it is not a straight gender issue). The reception varies greatly, hostility is rare: more common is a range from a degree of apathy through to keenness.

Where people are going to college and family is being involved then I do need to meet with people and share financial arrangements along with all the above – people need information to make good decisions.

The way that clergy couples experience the early stages of the process differs widely. Some feel almost joined at the hip, as though it were a joint vocation, although one bishop is reputed to have remarked, when told of such an attitude: 'I have searched the ordinal from end to end and nowhere can I find any mention of the spouse being ordained at the same time as the candidate!' Nevertheless some husbands do think in exactly those terms:

I was totally involved in her decision to offer herself for ordination. Having worked together in ministry for 11 years before she began to explore this new direction, we were intrinsically linked.

Others see themselves as bystanders:

My wife gave up paid work when our first child was born in 1981. She then started a search by working in various charitable organizations trying to find a purpose. My role was to ensure that we were financially secure and that she could pursue whatever venture she felt moved towards.

And in one extreme and very sad case, where the husband declined to take part in the survey at all, his newly priested wife said:

My husband would probably say that he tries to think about just being married to me, rather than married to a priest: 'uncomfortable' would sum up how he feels with regard to the latter!

Meeting the DDO: things for you to do

- If you know of others who have been through the process, find out what it was like and what advice they may have about how to handle the meeting.

- Discuss your expectations with your wife in advance. Try especially to understand why you are being invited and what you are expected to contribute.

- Prepare any questions that may occur to you, especially practical ones that may be less on your wife's mind than the vocation itself.

- Agree with your wife how questions of disagreement, concern and fear will be raised, and by whom.

- Don't be afraid to ask questions at the meeting, or to seek a follow-up meeting if there are remaining areas of concern.

- Discuss the meeting afterwards with your wife and be open to explore areas of emotion, anger and disagreement that may have arisen.

- If you have any lingering reactions, but don't want to trouble your wife with them, find a trusted person in whom to confide.

3

The impact of divorce

If either of you have been divorced it will be necessary under Section 4.3 of Canon Law for a faculty to be granted before your wife may proceed to a BAP. The granting of a faculty is done by the archbishop on the recommendation of the diocesan bishop. Regardless of which one of you has been divorced, and regardless of your role in the divorce, it will entail the following process:

1 An interview with the bishop's advisor which you are both required to attend.

2 Investigations by the bishop's advisor, involving contact with the divorced spouse and others who may have known the situation, such as friends or relatives.

3 Assuming a positive report from the bishop's advisor, a meeting with the bishop, which you are both required to attend.

4 Assuming he is satisfied, a recommendation sent by the diocesan bishop to the archbishop.

5 The issue of a faculty giving permission for your wife to proceed.

It is an intrusive process. It is a long process. It is an unavoidable process. Even if it flows smoothly, it is likely to add many months to the sequence of events, in some cases delaying the start of training by a whole academic year. In some cases the process may break down altogether. This might be because the circumstances of the divorce strongly suggest that an application would be unsuccessful. In some cases, couples decide for themselves that reopening past wounds and, especially, the need for contact with previous spouses, would be simply too painful, and they make a unilateral decision to withdraw from the process.

It is not fun! The bishop's advisors do their best to soften the ordeal, but they have a job to do. A degree of public exposure is involved.

The couple may have tacitly swept the subject under the carpet. Even without such collusion, the whole topic may not have been discussed for a very long time and the circumstances may be largely forgotten. Even if the couple have been totally open about it, they may never have discussed it in relation to possible ordination.

People react to the process in different ways. Those with a happy disposition are able to smile at it, viewing it as the bureaucratic machinery of the Church of England in full pomp. Others are cynical, suggesting that it achieves little but extra work and unhappiness, asserting that the Church is simply covering its back, especially given the assumption that all involved are telling the truth. Understanding the reasons for the process at an intellectual level doesn't in itself stop it having emotional repercussions: some people become sad, angry, frightened, or carry a huge sense of guilt.

This requirement may open up old wounds for the two people directly concerned and potentially change the dynamic of their marriage. Remember, too, the other people who get drawn into it – the previous spouse, the family and friends who are contacted: they, too, may be destabilized. In short, the whole thing can feel impertinent or intrusive; it may be embarrassing, making public a sequence of events that happened a long time ago in another place.

But how does the process feel in practice? Two clergy husbands share their stories, first a case where the wife, a prospective ordinand, had been divorced:

> My wife and I didn't meet until long after the divorce. I had never met or spoken with her ex-husband and knew nothing about him. When we were preparing for our wedding, she told me a little about the circumstances, because she wanted us to go into our marriage without any secrets. I appreciated that, but I didn't see any need to go into it any more than that, either then or now. When the bishop's advisor came round, we probably discussed what happened in greater depth than at any other time. It hurt!

Even if it is the husband who has been divorced, not the prospective ordinand, the same procedures have to be observed, as another respondent explains:

> I had been divorced, albeit after only six months of marriage. I had to have a meeting with the bishop's chaplain, alone. After

that I had to have two references from people that knew me before and after my divorce. He also wanted to contact my ex-wife to confirm that my version was correct. Because I wanted no contact with her I had to speak to her mother to find her address so that he could talk to her. Next we went to have an informal chat with the bishop. This completed, my details all had to be sent to the Archbishops of York and Canterbury for their permission, which was positive. But I thought it funny that all my details went to the very top. And it wasn't me wanting to be ordained.

Some people do look seriously at whether it's actually worth the pain:

Because of the requirement for all exploring ordination to obtain a licence prior to formal training if divorced (which in our case was me), it forced us to strongly question whether the institution was an appropriate framework within which to exercise ministry. The jury's still out to a certain extent! The process involved a joint interview with an independent volunteer with social work/ counselling experience (who seemed somewhat embarrassed on occasion) and an interview/attempted contact by the diocese with the previous spouse. I'm still struggling with the latter.

Each of these examples followed a slightly different course, but the essentials were the same: an initial interview, further investigations including contact with the previous spouse, and an interview with the bishop. It had to be done; it took time, and was not a happy part of the process for any of the parties involved.

From the point of view of the bishop's advisor, it can't exactly be pleasant to have to visit a perfectly happy and stable couple and eviscerate their relationship! It must be recognized, however, that if in the future a minister is going to be preparing couples for marriage and, in particular, helping the bride and groom to understand their wedding vows, it is not unreasonable for the Church to expect her to support the stand that it takes on the sanctity of marriage. Sadly, in this litigious and prurient age where such matters are seen as fair game for the gutter press, it is inevitable that the Church, like any other organization, will do its utmost to follow due process, and make sure it is clearly seen to have done so. It is a fact that the Church's discernment of the right way forward relies almost entirely on subjective opinions, selective memories and the assumption that people will tell the truth about something that may have happened decades ago. Whether this way of addressing a delicate topic could be improved – whether indeed it reflects current attitudes – is of course open to discussion, but nobody can really be surprised if the Church adopts a fairly heavy-handed process to head off potential scandal and bad publicity. This is the way things work, and until it changes, there is no alternative on offer.

Need a faculty? Things you can do

- Nobody wants nasty shocks, especially after they have already travelled some way along the path. Make sure your wife discusses the possible need for a faculty with her vocations advisor sooner rather than later and finds out exactly how it will involve you both.

- Understand for yourself how you are likely to react, on the basis that forewarned is forearmed.

- Discuss with your wife the implications of the investigations that will take place, especially contact with a previous spouse, friends and relatives; and the possibility that some people in your current environment may need to be made aware of things that you would prefer to remain confidential.

- If either of you sense any reluctance to go through this ordeal, identify the point beyond which you are not prepared to go, and discuss the potential consequences for your wife's aspiration to be ordained.

- Be aware that it may be your past, not your wife's, which is the reason why she may end up not being ordained. Be prepared for some deep and possibly painful conversations.

4

The early days: ordination and beyond

—— ·◆· ——

It was an exciting and exhilarating time . . .

Honeymoon period? What honeymoon period? I hate it!

The priesting and ordination were painful and increased the space between us . . .

The cards have been taken down from the mantelpiece, the thank-you letters have been written, you've paid for the party after the ordination service. Now life starts to settle into a routine. Or does it?

In a sense it may be easier for your wife. She will be liaising with her training minister to map out a working agreement and she will be establishing a learning path for her ongoing training. She may be planning hard-skills days and academic coursework, while filling her diary with engagements, commitments to preside at services, appointments to meet the churchwardens, the head teacher of the church school and everyone else with whom she will be working. At a social level, too, she will be forging new relationships. Even if she hasn't had to change church for her first curacy, she will be a different person and will need to establish her new persona. In short, she will almost be starting again from scratch.

In the meantime, as we saw in the introduction to this book, she will be getting used to what it feels like to wear her collar, how people react to her when they see her in the street, recognizing signs of things that she will have to cope with, accepting that people who were simply friends before may now place her on a pedestal and see her differently.

If her curacy has entailed moving house, you may add several other dimensions of disorientation. She will be getting used to the new home, which may or may not be your own. When everyone else would be thinking about the curtains, the carpets, what to do with the garden, how to decorate the children's rooms – everything that can turn a house move from a source of stress to a time of joy – her focus will be elsewhere. While the congregation may be very welcoming and helpful, they are not yet friends, and indeed it may never be practical for them to become close friends. She will miss her old friends, and so may you. The telephone, email and texting only get you so far, when what you would really like to do is kick off your shoes, open a bottle or two and pour out your woes, have a cry, or perhaps a good laugh. At the very time you probably want that most, in the midst of personal upheaval, the very friends to whom you would previously have poured out your woes may now be out of reach. So those friendships, too, are likely to change, however much you have vowed that they will stay the same.

And then there are the children. They will possibly be going to new schools, leaving behind them their special friends and the security of known environments. By virtue of being the child of an ordained minister they may find it harder than normal to settle in and make new friends, because they may be seen as different. At the opposite extreme, care for elderly dependent relatives may be a particular issue at this time. Of course, this is likely to have been a consideration when the appointment was first being considered, but it is amazing how such things can, even temporarily, take second place amid the zeal and excitement of doors opening to a new life of ministry.

You will notice that in all of this, you, the husband, have hardly been mentioned. You may or may not have had to change jobs in order to be alongside your wife, but your routine will almost certainly change, even if you have already retired or are not working. One benefit of the three years of training, even if it has been non-residential, is that you will already have had to adapt your routines to an extent, but a new home, a new environment, a change of focus will bring this all into perspective. All the while there is a strong chance that you will be carrying a major part of the burden of setting up the new home, or adapting your existing home so that your wife can work, receive visitors, and perhaps hold meetings.

All this disruption and split focus, for that is what it is, may shake the foundations of your relationship. Your wife will be spending extensive amounts of time with members of the team, especially the training minister, where the creation of a close working relationship is critical, and where it is inevitable that she will be brought into confidences that you may not know about. There will be a spiritual dimension too, since she is likely to view as a given the need to establish those new working relationships on the basis of time spent in prayer and studying together. In short, and especially if you go out to work, she may spend considerably more time with her new team members than she does with you. You may find yourself asking whether there is another person in your marriage. Who is it? Is it Jesus? The training incumbent? The institution of the Church? One counsellor has put it in these terms:

> Essentially it is about bigamous vows, both taken in church, without the consciousness that while they are both religious and compassionate, it gives the priest 'two masters' simultaneously. I believe Jesus had a word or two about serving two masters. Therefore without coming into consciousness, each clergy couple feels it is something only they are feeling in their marriage, because they are unprepared for it. The central feeling is one of exclusion.

Without careful work, discussion and planning by you both, and without sympathetic support, it is unlikely that your marriage will come through this phase completely unscathed. This is not meant to be a downer, but there is a need to be prepared. With eyes wide open, sharing of diaries, planning of quality time, clear communication and the right support network in the background, this transition can be a positive experience, a time of growth and new opportunities.

Here are a few challenges:

For the clergy husband

- If you are feeling left behind, and perhaps feeling that your personal, emotional or spiritual needs are not being met, what opportunities are there for you to get involved, not as a doer, but as a net receiver?

- How much of this can you plan for by thinking ahead, and how much was it part of your discussions right at the beginning when your wife announced her intention to seek ordination?

For female clergy

- How can you ensure that you don't become so enmeshed in your new life that you ignore, abandon or take for granted your husband and family?

For the host congregation

- How proactive are you, along with the parish and the deanery, in understanding the real pressures that face the families of new clergy, especially newly ordained clergy? Is the wife just a new pair of hands on the ministry team, and her husband someone they hope will take over coaching the boys' football team, the work of the treasurer or some other task that badly needs some help?

For the diocese

- How proactive are you in offering help, following up on new appointments, making it clear where help is to be found before it is too late?

- If there is any sort of network or programme for clergy spouses, is information communicated by the organizers or must the husband go looking? And has that network or programme, if it exists, adjusted from a default setting that clergy spouses are female?

This all sounds very gloomy, which is a shame, because in most cases you will probably be as delighted and excited as your wife is as she puts on her collar and gets her sleeves rolled up in the service of God. It's a time to celebrate. Alleluia! But ignore the essentials of your personal life at your peril.

The journey: key points

It's a very long process

The journey from discernment of vocation to ordination will take years, and even then the training won't have finished. Your wife will need patience and so will you.

You are part of the journey

However much or little you decide to be involved, and to whatever extent you share your wife's faith and support her sense of vocation, you are part of her journey and it will affect you.

Some of what happens will baffle you!

The Church will ask your wife to go through an apparently endless succession of hoops involving a lot of paperwork and other things which may seem equally pointless. You could be on the receiving end of the emotional fallout from the process and it may disrupt your home life.

You will probably be interviewed for your wife's job

In most dioceses, it is normal for you to be asked to attend a meeting in your own home with a vocations advisor or director of ordinands, and you may wonder why you are being interviewed for your wife's job! If you are in a diocese where this is required, go with the flow because resisting it will simply frustrate you.

Been divorced? Or your wife? Prepare yourself: it won't be pretty!

If either you or your wife has been divorced, there are extra procedures that are intrusive and potentially painful. You will need a faculty under Canon Law, and the process may cause a long delay to your wife's progress. There's no avoiding this and you might as well accept it, or agree from the outset that your wife walks away from ordination.

Know where to find help

Establish your own support mechanism as soon as possible. If you are lucky, you won't need to use it, but the chances are that there will be times when a good friend outside the parish, a spiritual director, or the husbands or wives of other ordinands and clergy will provide the opportunity to share your own feelings, joys and frustrations and to pick up good ideas and develop your own coping strategy. Don't be alone!

Communicate, communicate, communicate!

There's a fine balance: it's your wife's journey not yours, but wherever possible, communicate with her, share thoughts, anxieties, successes, expectations and fears. Talk through the practical implications. Talk. Better still: listen.

Take it to God in prayer?

In this book, no assumptions are made as to whether you are a Christian, someone of another faith or have no faith at all. If it is part of your practice, however, pray continuously. Pray in support of your wife; pray for yourself; pray for both of you.

Part 2

CLERGY HUSBAND: WHAT DOES IT MEAN?

What is a clergy husband? Some people will think of you as a sort of benevolent Denis Thatcher or Duke of Edinburgh, in a perpetual haze of good will, occasionally mischievous, but solidly there, walking three paces behind your ordained wife. Others will think of you more as a surrogate 'wife', doing all the housewifely things for which your wife simply doesn't have the time or energy. Some will see you as a church resource by right though not by appointment, a sort of mirror image of stereotyped views of a clergy wife. Yet others will assume that the two of you are partners in some sort of joint ministry, regardless of whether or not you are trained, ordained or even interested. Still others simply don't care, possibly reflecting an apathy or even hostility that you as the clergy husband may share.

Each of these caricatures may portray some truth, which only serves to prove that there is no such thing as a single model for a clergy husband. Some contributors to this book disputed whether it should even be published, citing their belief that there is no difference between a clergy husband and a clergy wife, and that to focus purely on clergy husbands is simply to perpetuate old prejudices, traditions and perceptions about female ordination.

What images do clergy husbands project? We have seen that we are largely spectators to our wife's journey to ordination and unless we ourselves are ordained, we do not have any specific, formalized role as she enters each phase of her ministry, regardless of the expectations and assumptions that some congregations may heap upon us.

When we come to think of our beliefs, the basic principles that drive us, the way of life lived in the shadow of the Church, and how we blend all of that with our personalities and, yes, our relationship with our wives, it can be argued that nobody is going to care more about us than we ourselves. It is my view that your starting point in exploring the life and work of a clergy husband must be yourself: who you are, how self-aware you are, and how much of yourself you are able to share.

Part Two deals with the following topics:

- The need to know and nurture yourself in an environment where you are often likely to feel like an add-on or to have been placed uninvited into a role.
- The need to be realistic about your role vis-à-vis your wife's ministry and about your own, if any, in comparison with her official one.
- The minefield of boundaries, expectations and precarious friendships.
- Above all, the need to know yourself, and who you want to be.

5

Know yourself

'I'm an ENFJ. What are you?'

Anybody who has ever been on a management development or team building course will recognize this as one of 16 possible outcomes of the Myers-Briggs personality assessment. It is a tool used in many organizations to help individuals to build their knowledge of themselves and each other so that they may relate better to one another. If you have not come across Myers-Briggs, perhaps you have done the Enneagram, the Belbin team-role model, or perhaps the four colour quadrants of the Insights model. Love them or hate them, they do seem to crop up at regular intervals. I feel as if I have explored them all, and generally the results come out the same. What a surprise!

Some of us will also have been invited to plot our 'personal time line', usually as a drawing starting at birth and ending at the present day. This exercise brings out our life-changing moments, the people who have influenced us, occasions of joy or disappointment, success or failure. The exercise aims to provide a holistic view of who we are and how we got here, covering relationships, spirituality, emotions, our work life and anything else that may be a key contributor to who we are.

Are we better integrated and more effective as a result of doing these exercises? I believe so, although in my experience of doing them alongside other people, there is a paradox. Some people are fascinated by them and love doing them, but they possibly learn very little new from them, because they tend already to be pretty self-aware. Conversely, there are people who are prickly and resistant, do the tests through gritted teeth and are not very interested in the results. They could be the very people who might benefit most from the insights such exercises offer.

If we are to gain fulfilment and enjoy a smooth ride in our lives as clergy husbands, we are more likely to succeed if we are comfortable with who we are and have an understanding of our preferences and dislikes, our strengths and weaknesses.

I have been in my current congregation since 2002: I doubt whether many of its members could say they know me well enough even to scratch the surface of who I really am. This is not because I am by nature secretive, far from it. It is simply that like many church families, we are often reluctant to pry, and relationships are likely to remain at a superficial level. If we do get closer, it is often only when something goes wrong, be it illness, job problems or marital difficulties. In the pressurized life of a clergy husband, the perceived need to present a patina of serenity may cause us to prevent others from getting close to us.

For me, therefore, the answer to the question 'what is a clergy husband?' has to start with me, inside me, perhaps being rephrased to 'what and who is this particular clergy husband?' What about you? Here are some exercises that may help you find some answers.

> **IMPORTANT**
> If any of the following exercises or questions raise issues that you find difficult, GET HELP.

Two exercises for everyone

What's your story? How well do you know yourself? How honest are you with yourself about the realities of your life, spiritual or otherwise? The two exercises that follow may help you to answer those questions.

1 If you have ever done any of the personality type exercises described above and still have the results, reflect on what they mean for you now, not when you originally did them.

2 Even if you have done it before, create your 'life line'. Draw a long horizontal arrow on a large sheet of paper, with dates at either end, starting as far back as you can remember and finishing now. Plot along the line:

- the key events in your life
- the key relationships
- times when particular people influenced or helped you
- times of spiritual development
- times of breakthrough and of disappointment
- successes and apparent failures or setbacks.

Reflect on what this tells you about yourself in your current situation. Keep your life line handy, so that you can add the next big event or change.

Questions

The following is a list of questions for you to consider. You may find some of them irrelevant or silly, but please suspend your disbelief and give them a go.

Questions for clergy husbands

- How aware are you of your emotions: the life-giving ones like joy, creativity and love; and the destructive ones like anger, defeatism and stress?

- Are your own needs, spiritual or otherwise, being met, and how can you fill any gaps? Who can you turn to? Where is your support?

Questions for ordained wives

- How well do you know your husband's story? How relevant does it feel to your own journey?

- How sensitive do you think you are to issues that may not be immediately apparent?

- To what extent does your husband have the freedom and space to be a husband first and a clergy husband second?

A question for members of the host congregation

- How well do you really know the clergy husband? How much do you care? Do you see him as a person with needs, or is it possible that you sometimes see him only as someone to fill gaps in the organization, or someone to act as the message-taker when his wife is out?

Questions for the deanery, archdeaconry or diocese

- How are clergy husbands seen? As an extra ministerial resource? As a financial enabler of the Church's shift towards self-supporting ministry? As a distraction? Or are they simply not thought of at all?

- Are you on the lookout for signs that all is not as it should be, and are you able to recognize the need to provide support when it is most needed, usually long before trouble flares up?

Even if answering these questions makes you feel that the rest of this book may be of little use to you, I would suggest that before you give it to Oxfam, you might ask yourself if that is just your convenient way of avoiding some real issues that need to be addressed, whether for yourself or for others who may be exactly in that position. They may need the benefit of your listening ear and counsel, preferably without censure, but full of charity and concern.

Whoever you are, it *does* apply to you!

6

*Ordained ministry:
an ordinary marriage?*

In some senses, there is nothing that makes a clergy marriage different from other marriages. All marriages require the couple to work out the ground rules, to learn to communicate and to negotiate. 'For better, for worse, for richer, for poorer', they have to go through times of great joy and mutual fulfilment, but also of tension, of temptation and perhaps of sorrow. Finance, or the lack or misuse of it, rears its head at some time in most marriages. As the couple get older, the physical passion of the early days may give way to a more settled relationship which in turn may lead to easy-going, loving companionship into old age. Career successes and disappointments, the need to move home, the impact of children or the lack of them, of good health and illness, maybe time spent caring for ageing parents, are common to all marriages. There are momentous decisions, career switches and opportunities, and for those blessed with a faith, the journey to self-knowledge travelled in harness with God.

This journey is common to all, yet unique for each couple. There has to be communication and negotiation for these turbulent waters to be navigated successfully, and it would be unusual if there were not times when the needs, desires or aspirations of one person require patience, understanding and sacrifice from the other.

In that sense, therefore, a clergy marriage is indeed just like any other. This book is not about all marriages, however, and this chapter is therefore a very short one, because what follows is an argument that clergy marriages, and especially those where it is the wife who is ordained, are different in particular ways, creating special challenges for both parties, and facing the clergy husband with a wide range of issues to think about and discuss, including some needs which may be counterintuitive.

Read on!

7

Ordained ministry: just another job?

———•◦•———

> Most of the issues that I have heard comments on are no different to those that occur in the business world in which I work.

Some clergy husbands have suggested there is no difference between being married to a member of the clergy and being married to someone in any other profession. Perhaps that's how you feel, but whether your wife would agree is another matter. It is nevertheless a point of view, and one worth testing. The next exercise may help you to do this in a tolerably systematic way.

Exercise

The following statements relate to the life of your wife, or to your life as a clergy husband. This list, which is of course not exhaustive, nevertheless gives a flavour of the peculiarities of clergy family life. In each case, consider to which other professions and in which other fields the statement could also be applied.

❐ In order to be selected for training and ordination, she will go through faith-based positive discrimination.

❐ Her vocation cannot be proved but must be discerned.

❐ Her vocation must be recognized and accepted before training can even start.

❐ At her ordination, she will be required to promise to fashion her household in the image of Christ. That means you and the children!

❐ Once she has been ordained, further training is required for between three and six years before she is considered fully qualified.

❏ If she lives in a church (= tied) house, she can't make any significant changes without going through a lengthy faculty process.

❏ She will probably be required to use the home for church purposes, and the public areas, including the garden, will need to be presentable – no old socks or yesterday's washing-up lying around.

❏ She will be expected to have a wardrobe of space-consuming, expensive specialist clothing that can't double for social use.

❏ If she is self-supporting, she will have made exactly the same statements of obedience to the state and to the bishop, and may have made exactly the same commitments of time and effort and in all those senses may be considered to be on an equal footing with stipendiary clergy. Because she is self-supporting, however, she may not have access to the same tax benefits and allowances because she does not have any income.

❏ She will frequently be required to work in conditions of damp and cold in buildings inadequate to meet normal working conditions.

❏ She will be required to undertake work for which she is not properly trained, such as management of building work, planning applications and finance.

❏ She will regularly be exposed to intense emotion, pain and anger as she deals with people who have suffered bereavement, redundancy or other personal tragedy.

❏ She will be privy to confidences which she may not share with family members or, in many other cases, with anyone at all.

❏ Whether or not you go to church yourself, you will see your wife working and be exposed to what people think of her and her way of working.

❏ There will be times when she seems to be married to her work rather than to you. She will be considered to be available to everyone at all times, whether at the doorstep, being stopped in the street, or telephoned at inconvenient times.

❏ Beyond tight limits, she will not be free at weekends, even if you are, and she may only have days off when you yourself are working.

❏ Her regular days off may have to change, often at short notice, due to funerals and other unpredictable occurrences.

❏ The people she works with will mostly be volunteers over whom she has no formal control or responsibility, and whose competence may be totally unrelated to their enthusiasm!

❏ She will be expected to write creatively and speak engagingly week after week.

❏ She will be expected to radiate a love of people, and reflect God's love for them, even if she doesn't actually like them. And so will you.

❏ She may be responsible for the members of a congregation, but her evangelistic responsibility is equally the attraction of non-members.

❏ Her children will often be expected to reflect her calling, with angelic behaviour and encyclopedic knowledge of the Bible, and they may be subject to bullying or criticism.

❏ Whether or not she likes children, she will need to give the impression that she does. And so must you.

❏ She must be seen to relate to the elderly, who often form the majority of the congregation, even though she may find them difficult. And so must you.

❏ She must relate equally and with charity to people from different social, ethnic or educational backgrounds, some of whom she may find difficult. And so must you.

❏ She may need to demonstrate a public position on sexual orientation that might be at odds with her personal convictions.

It is certainly true that some of these statements are valid for other professions. Anybody in the armed forces, or farm workers, or boarding school teachers would recognize the issues relating to tied housing. Doctors or solicitors would recognize the extended and ongoing training. Counsellors would recognize the exposure to people in pain and the need for confidentiality. Even advertising executives might claim that they are less interested in existing customers than in attracting new ones. The sheer breadth of characteristics, however, could not be applied to any other single profession.

Perhaps most germane, many of these characteristics of your wife's work will affect you and your family just as much as they affect her, even if you are a non-believer, are fully absorbed in your own profession or think you are completely detached. Some of them may prove to be divisive, driving a wedge through the unity of the family. It is this last point that raises the biggest challenge. While many clergy families are blessed with problem-free lives, others are not.

Things to think about

- Which characteristics of your wife's job will affect you, your marriage or your family and require special consideration?

- If you are a member of the congregation, the parochial church council (PCC) or the wider Church, how much weight do you place on supporting the whole clergy family in their unique lifestyle?

- At the diocesan level, or at theological colleges, what could be done, beyond the academic, the theological and the ideological, to prepare the family fully for the realities of life in a clergy household?

- And something for everyone involved to think about: going right back to the beginning of the process, should these realities carry greater weight in the whole discernment and selection process, and should the views of the husband be more proactively canvassed?

8

Male? Female? What's the difference?

Just as God is our Father, so God is also our Mother.

(Julian of Norwich)

'Our God is a wonderful Father, isn't She?!' (Preacher at a wedding)

Why is this book just for husbands of female clergy and not for clergy spouses in general? We have already touched on this, and it is certainly a sensitive area for some people.

A lot has been written about clergy wives. Take your pick from fiction, autobiography, sociological studies, web sites and casual discussion. There seems to be a stereotype of a clergy wife, just as on television, clergy themselves are invariably portrayed as otherworldly, bumbling idiots or wimps. Some clergy wives do indeed conform to a pattern, while others lead totally independent lives. Until relatively recently, however, there was nothing to say or write about husbands of female clergy, because they simply didn't exist. An understanding of the nature, needs and characteristics of clergy husbands remains elusive.

Differentiators

Even though we should not generalize about clergy husbands any more than we should about clergy wives, there are some factors that differentiate their situations.

Opposition to female ordination

In some quarters, opposition continues to linger. Clergy husbands report sadness at witnessing the great unkindness their ordained wives endure. The husbands may become angry, defensive, want to do something about it, and will certainly be supportive of their wives in their wide range of emotions. Being married to male clergy brings none of this baggage: there may be many other areas of contention, but opposition to male clergy is a non-issue.

History

Whether we like it or not, there is a long line of history and received wisdom about what a clergy wife is. Even where the ordination of women has been greeted with joy, however, there hasn't yet been time for an equivalent set of assumptions to emerge about clergy husbands. That may be a good thing, and perhaps no generalized view will ever emerge. Whatever, it is certainly new ground.

Essential gender differences

Are we to deny that men and women are different? Biologically? Certainly. Emotionally? Many would say so. Certainly, the popularity of the book *Men Are from Mars, Women Are from Venus*, published shortly before the ordination of women was introduced, would seem to support the idea that clergy husbands are likely to differ emotionally from clergy wives. This sounds simplistic, but as one diocesan counsellor said: 'I have had very few husbands of clergy refer themselves for counselling, although that may also be because men are somewhat less inclined to refer themselves for therapy than women.' Similarly, the organization Broken Rites, which provides support for separated and divorced clergy families, has received only a handful of enquiries from males during the short time since they changed their constitution to reflect the ordination of women.

Fundamental gifts

Many who support the gifts of women to the Church celebrate the nurturing, caring aspects of femininity that add fresh dimensions to worship, to pastoral care, to working with schools and children or the elderly, to hospital and hospice chaplaincies. This may extend to an active maternal role in the home too, complemented perhaps by a conventional paternal role for the husbands, quite different from prevailing expectations of the roles in which a clergy wife would become involved.

Sources of income

About 60 per cent of newly ordained females are self-supporting, in the sense that they are independent of church funds except for the reimbursement of expenses. This is true for only about 35 per cent of men. You must decide for yourself whether you think this shift in the provision of clergy is strategically based or simply represents financial pragmatism. For many, the clergy husband is still the principal breadwinner, whether from continuing salaried income or from an occupational or state pension. He is effectively funding his wife's ordained ministry for the benefit of the Church.

Areas of vulnerability

Consider an evening service taking place in a church down a dark country lane. Does a clergy husband feel as relaxed about his ordained wife going alone to unlock the church, and potentially sitting alone in a dark building, as the clergy wife does about her ordained husband doing the same? Possibly, but there is certainly a dimension of vulnerability here that differentiates the concerns of male and female clergy spouses, something that may also affect relationships with congregants.

Assumptions

A stereotypical image of a clergy wife might assume involvement in the caring, nurturing or decorative aspects of life ... working with young women and children, the Mothers' Union, flower-arranging, church cleaning, home-making, entertaining on behalf of her ordained husband. Even if there is only a shadow of truth in this rather unenlightened view, then what are the equivalent assumptions for a clergy husband? Serving on committees in quasi-managerial roles like treasurer, on the buildings committee, doing fund raising, organizing men's fellowships, sporting activities for the children, barbecues? These roles may indeed provide fulfilment and make good use of the husband's skills and experience, but they still represent a stereotype, just a very different one.

If all this seems to present a rather dry analysis unsupported by hard evidence, then some quotations from the survey of clergy husbands may throw further light on the subject and demonstrate the absence of any clear model of what a clergy husband is, how he is seen by others, and the assumptions that people sometimes make about him:

> The world has yet to acclimatize to the role of women in the Church, let alone their spouses.

> While there is still a certain amount of work to be done in understanding the role of female clergy, there is even more to be done in understanding the role of a clergy husband.

The role and position is still looked on with curiosity.

It is sometimes difficult to take a step back when my wife is the centre of attention and congregations seem to want all her time, particularly after services.

I learned to make cakes – as vicar's wife! Good fun and much appreciated by church members.

She is my wife first and foremost and as her husband it's my role to help and support her vocation – she calls me her 'guard dog for God'. Sadly this often leaves me twiddling my thumbs whilst she is off doing church work.

I wash the cassock and surplice, prepare the meals and make the cakes for events. Oh, and answer the phone whilst she is out at work. Essentially, I am the hidden support network for my wife's ministry. She always says that if I didn't do what I do behind the scenes, she wouldn't be able to do what she does. We worked this through very early on in the training process and agreed this would be the way.

Clergy wives have been around a long time and often (through college at least) have many things in common – mostly children. And there's only so many times you can hear about a baby's development before your sanity starts to fail!

Huge pain from treatment of me and my wife from the church. Have to carry her stress as well. People react to me as if they were speaking to clergy.

Having to play 'second fiddle' when sometimes you would like to be 'leader'.

When some people find out that I am the husband of a priest they react to me in a different way to the way that they did before.

I have several times been called the 'vicar's wife' – which has always been far more embarrassing for the person who has used this phrase.

At Spring Harvest several years ago, there was a seminar for clergy spouses. I decided to go but could not get past the two 'bouncers' at the door. After much discussion they eventually let me in. When I entered, there were about 70 women in the room with three women leading the meeting – no men in sight, and you could hear a pin drop as I walked across the room to join in. There was no comment about why I was there so I asked, 'Is this the clergy spouses' seminar?' to which they replied, 'Yes.' So I said, 'Good, I am glad that I have found the right place. My wife is a minister and I am here to see what it is like to be a clergy spouse.' I did get some very strange looks and possibly some that were angry, but several ladies were very welcoming and helpful.

Take your pick from this deliberately long list of quotations. Even without knowing the people or the contexts within which they live, you can see that the only thing that they have in common is that there is no such thing as an off-the-peg clergy husband. It is not even possible to create a generic role description for a clergy husband, especially given that some people assert that there *is* no role other than being married to female clergy. What is clear, though, is that whereas there is a general understanding of the dynamics that affect clergy wives, often distorted by mythology, stereotypes and assumptions, there is little understanding of the dynamics for men married to female clergy. There is a lot of catching up to be done, and it is therefore far from self-indulgent for a book like this to focus purely on clergy husbands.

9

Her journey – your journey?

———◆•◆———

> Will you endeavour to fashion your own life *and that of your household* according to the way of Christ, that you may be a pattern and example to Christ's people?
>
> (Extract from ordination service, italics mine)

It is probable that most people could say little about what exactly their wives or husbands do when they go to work. My wife is highly supportive of my work as a specialist process improvement consultant, but I don't expect her to have anything more than a passing under-standing of what I do. In the nicest possible way, why should she? Where clergy marriages are concerned, however, it is important to recognize any expectation that you and your ordained wife will operate as a partnership, especially if those expectations are based on assumptions about the nature and depth of your faith, if any.

One aspect of the survey of clergy husbands was especially reassur-ing, if in its own way intimidating. This was the apparent certainty of faith with which many clergy husbands travel their journeys along-side their ordained wives. Some of them are in ordained ministry themselves, and many are in some form of lay ministry. The following quotation is typical of those husbands:

> I suppose first and foremost my wife is responding to a call from God and I wholeheartedly share her vocation – in fact I see myself sharing that calling – it is not her 'career', as distinct from mine.

For such people, the promise made in the ordination service stands a good chance of being delivered. It has to be said, however, that in several cases, the husbands declared themselves atheists or agnostics, and some were from other denominations or religions than the Church of Eng-land. Similarly, others felt completely detached from the whole thing. Does this mean that, in such cases, the ordination promise is destined for failure before it has even been uttered? Some would apparently think so. Others would suggest that the husband's commitment should be more thoroughly probed before a candidate is allowed to start training for ordination. After all, if marriage is intended 'for the mutual society, help and comfort that the one ought to have of the other . . . for better and for worse', considerable challenges may arise where the wife is a 'professional Christian' and the husband is anything but.

My view is that we should cut ourselves a bit of slack here, because few of us are actually 'super-Christians'. We often overlook the fact that the people that Jesus sent out were not first-class honours seminarians with gleaming teeth and unshakable faith, but ordinary people like you and me – well, like me, certainly – with few certainties, but with an underlying flame that would not go out. This is where a few Bible verses give me huge encouragement.

'When they saw him, they worshipped him; but some doubted' (Matt. 28.17). For me, this gives me the permission that I need to plough my own spiritual journey, to be me, not to try to be the mirror image of my wife's faith as she lives her life of ministry, both as an individual and as an ordained person.

There is further encouragement in St Paul's words: 'My strength is made perfect in weakness' (2 Cor. 12.9). I am Jewish by birth, and became a Christian in my early twenties. I never take my faith for granted, but constantly reappraise what it is that I believe. In my case, this means listening to doubts and questions and subjecting them to honest scrutiny. I therefore see these doubts and questions as positive. You may not share this particular perspective, but I believe that wherever you are in your faith journey, this sort of honest review can be a gateway to real spiritual growth. In the words of Francis Bacon: 'If a man will begin with certainties, he shall end in doubts, but if he will be content to begin with doubts, he shall end in certainties.'

You and your clergy wife may have become attached precisely because of your shared faith and the fact that each of you, in your way, has a calling to ministry. You may, then, be perplexed at the notion that any other existence could possibly work. You may be one of those who find doubt difficult, threatening even. If that is your situation, I suggest there are three risk areas to consider:

- Could the certainty of your faith and the way you communicate it actually create confusion and a lack of clarity as to who is the ordained minister in your household?

- Is there any sense in which you are playing a part that you may feel is expected of you? Do you accept the possibility of doubts and nurture them?

- Are you unwittingly putting pressure on your ordained wife by being such a paragon of spiritual perfection that you stifle her freedom to express her own doubts, questions and growth points?

For some readers these questions may seem especially relevant; for others, they may not arise at all. But it may still be helpful for everyone to take time out occasionally to become aware of anything unwelcome that may have crept in, readjust if necessary, smile and move on. Put another way, give yourself permission to be human and make space for real growth, spiritual or otherwise. If you do, it will be like a new beginning.

Some challenges for clergy husbands

- As a clergy husband, do you make the time and space to be yourself, to travel your own faith journey?

- Do you give your wife the space to travel her own journey?

- Are you aware of pressures to conform or to adopt a particular spirituality, and do you have a strategy for working round them?

- Where do you go to nurture your own spirituality?

And one for female clergy

- Does your profession, in every sense of the word, place pressure on your husband? However unconsciously, do you contribute to that pressure?

A challenge for the congregation

- Do you expect the husband of your clergy to be so holy that he is a surrogate minister? What is your justification for doing so?

And one for all of us

- How well do you know one other? To what extent do you give permission for all to be themselves, and do you consider spiritual doubt as a failing or as an opportunity?

10

Does it mean I have to be involved?

———•◆•———

So far, we have established very little about what it is to be a clergy husband, except that you can't generalize and the best advice is to be yourself.

It is natural for people in your wife's church to take stock of your talents, experience and abilities and try to get you involved too. However much they may protest to the contrary, the opportunity to get two for the price of one will seem almost irresistible. You can hardly blame them for trying, but that doesn't mean that you have to capitulate: you have a choice.

Following her ordination, my wife was appointed as assistant curate at the church of which we were already members, and in which I was involved on several fronts. I was a member of various groups and committees, including the PCC; I had several leadership roles and was on the rotas for a number of other activities. I was probably perceived as the more active of the two of us, especially as Miriam had been all but invisible during her two years of training. She does not seek prominence and certainly doesn't have a taste for committees!

Now, returning as a deacon, Miriam was in the public eye and had authority conferred on her by her ordination and by her office. As important as the actual work, though, she was a changed person, both in herself and as perceived by others, and would need to establish herself anew. The impact of this appointment, especially the reconstruction of existing relationships, was at least as complex as if she had had to move to a new parish with no baggage and no previous history.

I decided that my first priority was obviously to be available to her as a support and encouragement. I took the view that she needed space to establish herself in her own right, no longer under the shadow of my high-profile involvement. I therefore went through all the things I had been doing and stood down from virtually all of them.

Everyone's take on this is different and some people suggested at the time that I hadn't needed to take such a drastic step. Several months later, however, I am certain that this was the right decision. It was my choice, but it is not always that simple. How does a chartered accountant, for instance, make a measured decision whether or not to accept the hand of welcome when offered a pivotal financial role on the church council, almost before the removal vans have departed?

> I'm quite surprised that I have ended up being the parish treasurer after saying that I wouldn't do it again. How do these things happen?!

I'm not sure I would have jumped in so quickly in the same situation. But it is not easy, and it must be for you to work it out for yourself, and to negotiate it with your wife, since your involvement is likely to have an impact on her professional life.

The first priority of the church should be to respect the clergy family's need to settle in. In some churches it is actually the practice to stand in the way of someone offering himself or herself for office until that person has had time to settle in. This approach can be a response to the perceived need to test the person's mettle and commitment, or can equally arise from an altruistic desire to meet the incoming family's personal and spiritual needs first, and only take advantage of their gifts later.

Every husband, every church, every situation is different and this book cannot tell you what to do or what is appropriate in each case. Here, though, are a few points to think about:

For husbands

- On the assumption that you support your wife's ministry, what are your priorities as she settles into her new role and you settle into your new surroundings or lifestyle? Don't be afraid to stick up for your needs.

- If you feel moved to offer your services, or indeed you are invited to do so, what is the potential impact on your family life and especially on your wife as she settles into her ministry? Others may not understand the possible knock-on effects.

- Do you have a conviction that what is being asked of you, or what you are offering, is what God wants, or that the timing is right? Be prepared to listen and discern, and to take any decisions in a measured way.

- How will you feel if the church simply doesn't want your contribution, whatever your skills and however glittering your successes in previous congregations? How will you deal with this, should it happen?

For ordained wives

- If your husband offers to get involved in some way, has he discussed it with you? Have you shared your feelings on the matter? Have you been brave enough to suggest that he hang back if that feels the right thing?

- If your husband has been part of your ministry before, are you sure that that is what is required now? Are the parish aware that you 'come as a package'? Do they recognize his ministry alongside yours? How will you, too, feel if they don't want his contribution?

For congregations

- Do you have expectations of the clergy husband?

- Do you see his skills and experience as yours of right?

If you answered 'yes' to either question, have a really good think about why, and whether it is fair.

- If the incoming clergy husband offers specialist skills that are already catered for within the congregation, how will you turn down his offer in a way that does not leave him feeling rejected?

- Conversely, if he will clearly fill a yawning skills gap in the church, how will you decide when or if to involve him, and how will you balance that against his need to settle in, just as any other person would after moving house, changing job or joining a new congregation?

For dioceses and deaneries

- How much are the needs of the whole clergy family taken into account when overseeing new appointments, and how much guidance is given to parishes about the appropriateness of involving clergy husbands?

11

Boundaries and expectations

Let's be quite straight about it. Whatever your expectations, as a clergy husband there will always be an extent to which boundaries impede your involvement and relationships, and your ability to communicate freely. The following examples give a flavour of the barriers you may come across as a clergy husband.

Between you and your ordained wife

This is perhaps the most pernicious, and perhaps unexpected, boundary. Your wife is the one who has been ordained and is in a leadership position. This may run completely contrary to other aspects of your married life, or of your professional life where you may now or in the past have been in a senior managerial position. You need to be realistic and accept it; otherwise you may find yourself facing the sorts of problems discussed in Part Four of this book. Even at her ordination, it is your wife who promised to 'form herself and her home in the image of Christ'. This may manifest itself in a number of ways:

- She will seem to be spending more time in the church than at home.

- When she is at home, it may be difficult to know whether she is on church business or family business.

- She may expect to use the home as an extension of the church.

- She may develop deep working relationships with other members of the clergy team – perhaps seeming to be closer to them than to you.

- She will spend large amounts of time counselling, supporting and giving pastoral support to members of the congregation. You are unlikely to be invited!

- If she is deeply spiritual and you are not, it could seem as if Jesus is 'the other man'. That may be true to an extent for any clergy husband, but how much more so, how bleak, for the person of little or no faith at all, like a wedge being hammered steadily into the foundations of your marriage.

- You will have different routines, and it is quite possible that you may go days at a time without sitting down to eat a meal together, and even that may be constantly interrupted by the telephone.

- She will be privy to confidences that she can't share with you. If she tells you things that she has learned in confidence, she is in error.

- You will nevertheless become aware of some things that you can't talk about outside the home, which you may find pressurizing.

If you are experienced, you can no doubt add to this list. It is a fact of life when you are married to an ordained person that your wife's way of life, her spirituality, her relationships and the way she spends her time may create all sorts of barriers. It is clear from the survey that, fortunately, not everyone finds this difficult to cope with, but for others it can be a problem. It's not something that can be left to chance.

Between you and the clergy team

If you have concerns, spiritual doubts, anxiety about possible illness, professional problems or even marital difficulties, who are you going to take them to? Are you as free as an 'ordinary' member of the congregation to talk to the clergy?

If your wife is the vicar, you effectively do not have an independent, emotionally detached person with whom to share the very issues that may already be troubling her anyway. And if your wife is still in her first curacy, the vicar is likely to be her boss. In such a situation, you are little better off if the problems with which you are wrestling impinge on your wife's career.

So what about clergy in a neighbouring parish? Whoops: they are colleagues of your wife, so how much are you really going to tell them? Will the rural dean be in any better position to help you? Sounds lonely, doesn't it?

Between you and the rest of the congregation

We will talk about friendships in the next section, but just consider the following factors which may influence or impede your relationships within the congregation:

- By virtue of being married to a member of the clergy, you are already seen as different.

- People may assume that you are a person of faith and that you possess Bible knowledge equal to that of your ordained wife. No pressure then!

- They may expect you to come to church regularly and consider that you are disloyal if you do not.

- They are likely to use you as a conduit for giving feedback to your wife, however many times you advise them to talk directly to her. This may include using you to give sideswipes, criticisms and complaints.

- When they talk to you, they may expect you to know everything that your wife knows about, even though you may have absolutely no role in the church and the things they expect you to know are actually confidential.

In the face of these boundaries, assumptions and expectations, how on earth can you expect to be 'just another member of the congregation', even if that is what you want?

Where's the evidence?

You may be the sort of person who never gets stressed or bothered. Indeed, these boundaries may be exactly what you expected when your wife offered herself for ordination. The following respondents to the survey, though, suggest that these barriers can be real and painful, especially if unexpected:

> There was the general sense of my wife enjoying a life separate from my own which I was little part of.

> Knowing that she is carrying something that bothers her and having to accept that she cannot share.

> Although my wife would deny it, I am no longer the most important thing in her life. It is particularly difficult if the most important person in her life is someone I can see only as an imaginary friend.

> I think we share a bit less – not much, but as my wife is often told things in confidence I do not get to know and as we shared everything this is quite a change.

All right, you may feel that some of these people should face reality, but for them perception is reality.

Strategies for dealing with barriers

Take a lead in ensuring that days off, holidays and at least mealtimes are protected. Miriam and I go through the diary once a quarter and book monthly 'dates'. It's the only way we can guarantee that we are in the same place at the same time. The rules are that church business and my work (including writing this book!) are off limits. Walks, meals together, games of Scrabble and sitting on the sofa in front of a romantic movie are very much on the agenda. Might something like this work for you? Maybe not, but you can be proactive here in addressing the boundaries between you and your wife.

If you are a person of little or no faith, that is to be respected. You were married 'for better or for worse'. You need to be able to talk about it with your wife in a non-confrontational way. My experience is that bottled-up resentment results in an explosion, whereas appropriately timed conversations, however difficult, can forestall far greater difficulties. This may need you to be generous or brave: someone has to take the lead in saying 'sorry' or recognizing that a gulf has opened between you.

Develop a network of friends that you trust and people you can share your problems with before they come to a head. I have a spiritual director and one or two trusted friends in other parishes. In my diocese there is a well-publicized way of finding a spiritual director (or soul-mate, or buddy – the name doesn't matter, the relationship does). Perhaps this may work for you, or perhaps there may be someone else. Don't be alone.

Find your own sources of spiritual sustenance. Mine include the Cursillo movement, membership of a men's breakfast in a different parish, Fr Richard Rohr's daily email meditations, Bach and jigsaw puzzles. Yours might be Spring Harvest, New Wine, Greenbelt, Ignatian retreats, museums, concerts, the allotment or something similar – or indeed quite different. A friend of mine occasionally takes time out to 'go to a proper service' at Westminster Abbey.

Finally, if you are reading this and you are not a clergy husband, you may be feeling a bit like an interested onlooker and thinking that this has nothing to do with you. The fact is, however, that through your role, your way of life or natural forces, you may be the very cause of some of these barriers, unwittingly piling brick upon brick until that clergy husband has become a stranger to you. Some of the barriers are inevitable and cannot be removed. But wherever possible, it is up to everyone to play their part in recognizing them and minimizing their power.

12

Church attendance

If you go to church regularly, it may seem odd to you that some clergy husbands might not want to or be free to do so. Similarly, if you feel it normal to accompany your wife as she officiates at, say, four Sunday services from early morning through to lunchtime, involving travel across a widely scattered rural benefice, you may be bemused that other clergy husbands don't automatically do so.

If that is you, it might be tempting to skip this chapter, but it is not quite that simple. There may be others in your circle who don't see things the same way that you do, and it may be worth sticking with it, if only to get an insight into their view of life. The same applies if your view is quite the opposite and you would never usually go to church at all for whatever reason, whether through a lack of faith, adherence to another faith or simple apathy! Either way, it is worth taking this seriously.

Even if you are a person of faith – and this book makes no assumptions – it is your decision whether you go to church at all, go to the same services at the same church as your wife, or go to all of the same services in which she is involved. The decisions families take about worshipping together, especially if there are children involved, should be treated as private decisions, regardless of your wife's leadership position or indeed your own if you have any.

When it comes to worship patterns, one of the less agreeable aspects of being part of a church household is that we may face expectations from at least three different sources – four if you include God. I don't actually see him as a sort of class monitor standing at the church door checking everyone in and tut-tutting if people are not there. It saddens me when I meet people who share that view of God, and even more so when I encounter churches that seem to teach that 'miserable worm' outlook from the pulpit, but since I am not qualified to preach on differing doctrines of salvation, let's not go there!

If we leave God out of the equation, however, there remain three potential sources of expectation, as well as some that are simply imagined. These are the congregation, your ordained wife and you, the clergy husband.

Self-imposed expectations

Let's start with the expectations you yourself impose, because it is entirely possible that any others may simply be projections of your own feelings of 'should' and 'ought'. These are two of my least favourite words in church vocabulary, especially when preceded by the word 'we', which generally means 'you'!

I know that I don't actually have to go church simply because my wife is a curate or because she is actively involved in a service. Similarly, when she is involved in two consecutive services, I certainly don't need to go to both of them. That doesn't stop me feeling uneasy, as if I were in some way letting her, the church or myself down. I am fortunate: I don't sense any particular expectations from my wife or from the congregation, so this uneasiness is self-imposed. It's not as if I were so intensely religious by nature that I feel an irresistible urge to be there for every last minute. It's just that I have a huge capacity to feel guilty about things!

This is not to suggest that a sense of conscience is in some way bad; but let there be a distinction between a consciously thought through approach to church attendance, and a guilt-driven and destructive slavishness.

The congregation's expectations

It may be that the congregation considers that every properly functioning clergy family should attend every service. They may seem to take careful note when you, an ordinary person just like them, take Sunday off, miss one of the services or – shock horror – take your children to one of those non-church activities that increasingly seem to happen only on Sunday mornings. They may communicate their feelings in a variety of ways . . . to your face, whether directly or with sarcasm, using your wife as a conduit, or through that robust rival to the parish magazine, the grapevine. It could be, however, that Mr Smith's enigmatic look actually means that he is worried whether the frost got his early lettuces, or that Mrs Jones' frown is really the result of the pain in her arthritic hip.

To the clergy husband

- Choose what you are going to do, and stick to your decision. Don't see hidden meanings in every glance, and trust the congregation and the leadership team.

To the congregation

- Don't apply standards that you wouldn't apply to yourself! The clergy husband and the children are on their own journey.

Your wife's expectations

Your wife may expect you to put in an appearance reasonably regularly. Whether or not she has a right to that expectation reflects the sort of marriage you have, so discuss it from the outset, and renegotiate it each time your wife moves to another church. It may be, however, that you are imagining the expectation.

To the clergy husband

- Listen, communicate with your wife; understand what it is that she is looking for and what she may really be asking of you, which may have nothing to do with whether or not you go to church. And be aware that you may be imagining expectations that don't exist.

To the ordained wife

- If you have expectations, state them clearly and be prepared to come to an agreement, especially if you rely on your husband to transport you to all your Sunday services, or assume that he will manage child care while you are busy up front. He is on his own journey and needs his space. And if he is imagining expectations that you don't have, gently tease him!

A possible risk: impact on your wife's image

Even if we put all these expectations to one side and you have the strength of character to do what feels right for you, there is another factor to consider. People have a funny way of making value judgements about clergy based not just on their performance in the role, but also on what is noticed about their family, lifestyle and much else that is frankly no one else's business! So, if you don't go to your wife's church, people may add two and two together and make forty-seven . . .

It may be assumed you and your wife have had a row, or that you are disloyal. Perhaps she is seen as setting a bad example of Christian family life, or you are having a faith crisis. Or, it may be said, if she can't influence her family, why should we take any notice of her?

Take your pick or add your own! However unfair they are, any of these assumptions may have an impact on your wife's image. Whether or not you let that influence your worship pattern must be up to you, but do be aware of the potential consequences.

Conclusion

In the matter of how you as a clergy husband decide when and if and where and how frequently to go to church, remember above all that you do indeed have a choice. Others, including your wife, may indeed have expectations and assumptions, but you have no need to apologize: the far greater priority is for you to be true to yourself.

13

Friendships and relationships

So, you are married to a newly ordained curate. You have just moved in and are getting to know people. Perhaps you strike up a rapport with some of them: you find that one person shares your tastes in music, another does the same sort of work as you, and you keep bumping into a third while you are walking the dog or on the school run. Maybe you think about inviting them round for a coffee, or they invite you for a meal.

It all sounds perfectly normal until you consider that any of these people, whether now or in the future, may be your wife's work colleagues (ordained and lay, paid and unpaid), part of your wife's wider organizational hierarchy, or a recipient of your wife's public ministry or one-to-one counselling.

Let's add another dimension. These same people may like or dislike your wife. They may think she's good or bad at her job. They may have the ability to influence her career, for good or bad. And they are quite likely to comment publicly about her, both positively and negatively.

When you combine these rather formidable lists, you may then be faced with questions such as these:

- Is it possible for these people to satisfy the criteria for being a real friend?

- Will your wife welcome seeing them socially or may it create a conflict for her?

- If you befriend them, will other people be jealous and stir up rumours of favouritism?

- Which will come first, loyalty to your wife or their friendship?

- Should the need arise, for your wife's professional or pastoral reasons, would you be prepared to distance yourself from them?

These questions apply when moving to a new parish, when everyone is new. They become all the more searching if your wife's first role is in the church of which you were already members, for then there is a sense in which every relationship needs to be reassessed. However close people may previously have been, the fact that your wife's relationship with them is now on a professional footing is sufficient to make you consider whether those friendships can stay the same. Be aware that making this adjustment may cause sadness, resentment or anger, both for you and for your friends.

Some people do not find this a problem, so it's important to say that this is not a prescription for having no friends in your wife's parish: far from it. After all, one of this book's key messages is 'don't be alone'. Somewhere there is something that will work for you, so here are a few thoughts.

Thoughts for the clergy husband

- Protect for as long as possible those friendships and relationships that you value. Take the initiative in maintaining contact. Phone, write, set up an internet video call. Arrange to meet regularly.

- Talk with your wife about how to handle relationships within the congregation and with her team. She may be relaxed about it.

- If you actively nurture your spirituality but feel unable to form close relationships within your wife's congregation, consider getting involved in an activity elsewhere, perhaps a men's fellowship in another parish.

- Make sure you have activities that reflect your own interests. These may give rise to new friendships.

Thoughts for the ordained wife

- Remember that while you are busy creating new professional and pastoral relationships, your husband and children may be floundering. Give them time to catch up. If they seem to be resentful, talk about it.

- If you need your husband to keep somebody at a distance, explain it clearly. Try to spot the signs and don't let the friendship develop too far, as the longer it is allowed to last, the worse the fallout may be.

Thoughts for the congregation

- Understand that the clergy husband is not being standoffish if he doesn't seem to want to get too close. Consider what it would be like if your own spouse started being friends with your work colleagues.

- When you phone the vicar's or the curate's home and you get her husband instead, remember that he is exactly that – in most cases he is not an ordained person.

- Try to behave with the clergy family as you would with any other family. They are people first and foremost. They are not super-human, and they have the same needs and frailties as the rest of us.

Clergy husband: what does it mean? Key points

———◦•◦———

Know yourself

You are an individual in your own right, not part of a package. Your life as a clergy husband is more likely to be happy and trouble free if you have a degree of self-knowledge and self-acceptance.

You and your wife are not joined at the hip

She has her vocation, and so do you, spiritual or otherwise. To assume that you are by right part of her journey or profession could be intrusive. You have your own journey to travel, and so does she.

It isn't easy!

People make assumptions, create expectations and may put you on a pedestal. They may underestimate the subtle pressures of being a clergy husband, the difficulty of confronting boundaries and confidentialities while still remaining friendly. It's hard for the clergy, and equally hard, but perhaps less recognizably so, for the clergy husband.

This job is different

You may think it is just like any other marriage or any other job. Ask yourself: is that straight denial of the reality of the situation, or a carefully thought through and discussed response to the new way of life?

Communicate and negotiate

One thing that may stand seriously in the way of settling in to life as a clergy husband is reluctance to communicate and negotiate. It isn't always easy, but it's usually worth the pain and effort: that is how understanding emerges and how log-jams can get shifted.

Exercise

When your wife joined her present church, she will have written a working agreement governing her relationships, her involvement, her working hours, the way expenses would be handled and so on. Create an imaginary working agreement or role description for yourself as a clergy husband, perhaps using the headings in this section as prompts. When you are ready, talk it over with your wife.

Part 3

LIFESTYLE ISSUES

We have now developed an understanding, perhaps based on personal experience, of the journey that our ordained wives have embarked on and continue to travel, and we have looked at the need to form a clear understanding of who we are as individuals and as clergy husbands. We need to add a third element into the mix, the practical everyday issues that are part of every family's life, but which in some senses affect clergy households especially.

In this part of the book we look at:

- the impact of living in a clergy household, whether or not the home is owned by the Church;

- the financial implications of clergy life, especially where the ordained wife is self-supporting;

- how we can ensure that communications, telephones and emails don't tyrannize our lives;

- how, amid all the noise, we can maintain quality of life and protect the interests of the family.

14

The home

---◆---

Forget the *house* for a moment, and think of the home. In many ways, it doesn't matter whether you live in a large, draughty, church-owned vicarage in a state of dilapidation, in a state of the art church house, or in your own family home. There is much to think about, wherever you live. Be prepared for life in a goldfish bowl!

Factors affecting all clergy homes

You are living above the shop. Your wife works from home, and these days that is very common for one or both partners in a marriage. Unlike many of those other situations, however, there is a huge amount of ambiguity as to whether or not your wife is on duty and therefore whether at any particular moment she is seeing the house as a home or as an office, and this is likely to affect you. This ambiguity may manifest itself in a number of ways.

The clergy home may be assumed by some to be also a church office, available to all. In addition, some people may consider your wife to be available and on duty round the clock, and so may she. Is she at home or at the office? People in other professions can generally close their study door and consider themselves off duty. Your wife cannot put it all down in quite the same way.

The telephone may ring for her anywhere in the house – more of telephones and emails in Chapter 16. People, known and unknown, may appear at the front door at any time of the day or night. Your wife may not be wearing a collar, but she is perceived to be available. If she is not, it is seen as her fault, and yours too! Issues of confidentiality will abound, as already discussed.

People may need to come to the house for counselling, or your wife may decide to hold church meetings in the house. You may actually have a choice – I have known clergy who held no meetings at home, but used church premises for all meetings – though she may not be able to avoid this, and indeed she may not wish to. But her study may not be big enough or appropriate for some of these events, in which case they may spill over into other parts of the house, affecting you and the family.

Most people working from home do so in physical isolation from their colleagues, to the extent that they could work all day in their pyjamas, surrounded by the last week's washing up! The fact that others may need to visit in connection with your wife's work may create expectations of tidiness that may be unfamiliar or uncomfortable for you and the rest of the family. You may need to consider potential ambiguities where rooms are used both by the family and for church purposes. Is it always appropriate for family photographs and ornaments to be on display in rooms used for church-related activities?

It is true that anybody working from home may need times when Charlie isn't playing his electric guitar or drums, or when you are not making a racket with the electric drill (sorry for the stereotypes!). For most, however, there is a semblance of working hours. Having to be quiet and invisible because there's a prayer meeting going on downstairs is not necessarily what you signed up for when you got married. And inspiration doesn't have a timetable: there may be times when your wife has to go and write down that perfect phrase for her sermon.

Then there are the silly things . . . When can you hang your washing out, and is it acceptable for the vicar's underwear to be visible on the washing line? What about sitting in the living room having a cuddle when anyone passing might see? You will be able to think of equally bizarre examples, but what is seen as unremarkable for 'normal' people can create outrage when clergy families do exactly the same thing. And what about the adorable cat or the darling dog that may start church visitors wheezing because of allergies or cowering with fear in the corner? It doesn't mean that you can't have pets: far from it – it's your home. But it's yet another thing that differentiates your home from 'ordinary' homes and needs to be thought through.

Church-owned houses

I do enjoy living in a house that is larger than we could afford and allows me a separate work space and a good sized garden.

I wish I had known how cold church houses can be.

Some people describe living in a vicarage in the most positive terms, relishing the luxury of having a large house for the first time. It is also true that many vicarages were purpose designed, with segregated working space for the clergy and convenient cloakrooms. There may be some financial advantages: depending on where you live, some of the costs, telephone lines, council tax, utilities and insurance may be covered in full or in part. Even in working conditions which may be ideal for your wife, however, there are factors that will affect how you live.

Although the house may have been newly decorated when you moved in, it was probably not done to a high specification because of lack of funds. You may have had little choice over the décor, and the paintwork and walls may have had inadequate preparation. I saw a vicarage once where peeling back the wallpaper was like an archaeological dig! If the house is furnished, you may find yourself inheriting a motley assortment of items which you wouldn't choose in a million years.

A large vicarage may be cold and draughty, and without double glazing. You may be stuck with expensive heating bills just to be comfortable, especially if you hold meetings for which people may expect a higher temperature than you are normally obliged to endure.

If you want to make any alterations in the house or garden, you may need a faculty from the diocese when many other householders could just get on and do it. This will add hassle and delays, and you may end up doing all the paperwork if your wife is too busy to get involved. What's more, when you move you won't see any capital benefit from improvements that you've funded, even though you may enjoy a better quality of life while you are there.

The garden may have been maintained to a standard which you find hard to emulate. Others may nevertheless expect you to keep it looking tidy and attractive. Indeed the church may have made this an explicit requirement, and this may influence how and when children and pets can use the garden. Since when were green fingers a requirement for ordained ministry?

Above all, this is not your house. If your wife leaves her ministry for any reason, or when she retires, you will be homeless unless you have been able to make other provision: just one point, but a critical one. More of this in Chapter 15.

Your own house

If living in a vicarage or church-owned house has its problems, there are other considerations to living in your own home as your wife exercises her ministry. It will not have been purpose-built, and unless you are lucky, it will not have a ground-floor office, with adjacent cloakroom, where your wife can work and receive visitors without potentially disturbing the rest of the household or making them aware of the emotions and confidentialities that often accompany such visits. Because of this lack of discrete working space, it may be necessary for you to be out when certain things are happening, or else to be invisible and quiet.

Your lounge and/or dining room may have to double as a meeting room, and you and the family might have to go and watch the television or relax elsewhere.

> The arrangement of our present house means that the piano is in the hall, so if a church group are in the sitting room I can't use the piano.

It may be harder to keep the house as a place that people can visit. Some people have a routine of daily dusting and vacuuming, but if you are both busy, who is going to do that? In any case, you may be comfortable living to less rigorous standards:

> Once when I had neglected the vacuuming my wife had a caller so she quickly vacuumed the hall and stairs up to the corner knowing that her guest could not see beyond that. Whilst praying quietly they were interrupted by a shout from our oldest son as he arrived home: 'Mum, why did you only vacuum half the stairs?!'

Any ambiguity about whose territory this really is will probably be even more acute in your own property than in a vicarage, especially if your ordained wife is in part-time or self-supporting ministry and perhaps holding down a busy job.

The home: things to think about

Is your house a home? Is it an office? Is it a church hall? Is it a private place or in the public domain? Here are some ways of approaching the many questions involved, whether you are living in a church-owned or privately owned house.

- Make sure that part of the process of choosing a parish includes establishing a clear understanding of the living arrangements, standard of decoration, responsibility for upkeep of the garden, expectations for how the house will be used and everything else we have explored in this chapter.

- Do make sure that your wife's assumptions are the same as yours. If not, start negotiating! In particular, agree the boundaries: which parts of the house are available for church use, which are strictly private, and when. Be prepared to stand up for the interests of the family – your wife may simply be too busy to give this sufficient attention. If necessary, be prepared to put your foot down. It's your home too! Remember: regardless of what your wife's predecessor did in the family home, whether church-owned or otherwise, and regardless of what expectations or assumptions may be expressed explicitly or otherwise, there is no obligation to open your home up in the same way.

- If you do make your home available for church use, it must be your combined, conscious choice, whether freely given as a gift to the church or as a sacrifice of service.

15

Finances

Money is one of the leading causes of domestic strife, sometimes leading to major disputes or even divorce. This is as true for clergy families as for the rest of the general population, even though some people may imagine that ordination somehow provides immunity against such worldly problems. Financial issues need to be addressed and understood.

Who pays the bills?

If you are the clergy or ordinand husband, you need to know what you are letting yourself in for financially! In Chapter 8, it was pointed out that about 60 per cent of newly ordained females are self-supporting: their gift is of themselves, at minimal cost to the Church. In many cases, your income or pension is the primary source of household finances that makes it possible for your wife to exercise her ministry. Even if she is in stipendiary ministry, her annual salary would be considered pretty miserable in most skilled professions – and an affront to some, vocation or no vocation – and probably insufficient to maintain a family without at least some additional income. Let's now consider some of the expenses specific to clergy life.

What has to be paid for?

Clerical clothing

Many clergy wear clerical clothing most of the time, and for services use anything from an all-purpose cassock and surplice to a fully comprehensive range of vestments reflecting all types of worship and the colours of the church seasons. Even those who do not wear vestments for services still wear clerical collars at least some of the time.

Your wife may have little choice if she is appointed to a church where the full range of vestments is expected. The good news is that upon ordination, there is generally a one-off grant available as a contribution towards vestments, and generous relatives and friends often wish to mark the occasion by contributing, either financially or with actual gifts. Some churches also have sets of the more expensive garments for the clergy to use. Nevertheless, you will need to agree how the following will be funded:

- day-to-day clergy shirts, collars, suits, etc., with regular replacements to keep looking smart and business-like;

- vestments for services, including cassocks, surplices, albs, stoles;

- the specialist laundering required for some items.

It may be worth finding out whether any of this expenditure is tax deductible, but that would only apply to those in stipendiary ministry.

Training

Ongoing training continues after ordination for a minimum of three years in the Church of England, and can last as long as six or seven. This will involve a mix of self-managed study, hard-skills days, on-the-job training, seminars, peer group meetings and conferences. Costs include:

- travel

- books, stationery and computer consumables

- courses with fees to be paid.

It is essential that you and your wife investigate what is paid for by the diocese or by the local church to avoid misunderstandings. You need to know the implications for the household budget.

Retreats

Many clergy regularly go on retreats. In some cases this is seen as an obligation. Many establishments bend over backwards to offer concessions, but they still come at a cost. The parish may contribute, but that cannot be guaranteed, so the household may need to fund retreat fees and/or travel to the retreat house.

Travel

With ministry teams covering increasingly large geographical areas, a car is generally vital. The family may even need to make the step change of buying a second car, with all the outlay of initial purchase, tax, insurance and running costs that entails. While the official mileage rate allowed by the Church is designed to contribute to running costs as well as fuel, the parish may not be able to afford it or may place limits on how much they will pay. A lot can be done on foot, and bicycles provide healthy exercise; a horse might be nice, but even they have to be fed! Seriously, your household budget needs to include:

- fuel;

- insurance, tax disc, MOT, repairs and maintenance;

- the cost of a second car if this is considered unavoidable.

'Will you have a cup of tea?'

How often do you think that question is asked in a year in clergy homes? And how often does that cup of tea come accompanied by a biscuit, or maybe some home baking? Perhaps there's a box of tissues on the side, too. At the risk of sounding petty, who pays for the tea bags, the jars of coffee, the milk, the sugar, the tissues and the loo rolls? You may consider all of this to be a normal overhead of financing a clergy household, or it may come as a complete surprise. Whatever, you need to build it into your calculations; and if there are frequent meetings in the clergy home with a tradition of refreshments, then this is something to be negotiated with the PCC . . . and with your wife!

Day-to-day running costs

Anyone who works from home needs to keep careful track of day-to-day expenses. This is sometimes complicated by expenditure that covers both personal and working use. Some costs may be claimable, whether reimbursed by the Church or as an offset against tax, but only if they are used exclusively for your wife's work. It may make sense, therefore, to ring-fence some equipment purely for church use, if for no other reason than to ensure that you are not unwittingly subsidizing the Church at the expense of family necessities.

Other financial considerations

There may be some circumstances in which the exclusive use of a room in your own property as a home office may qualify for a council tax discount. Check it out!

There may also be circumstances in which it is more efficient for the church, and possibly for you too, if you submit full claims for legitimate expenditure and increase your Gift Aid donations to the church. If you are a higher rate tax payer, the increased donation can be offset against your own tax allowance; the church benefits from the Gift Aid rebate, and you are no worse off. This gives the church a proper view of what it actually costs to operate on a day-to-day basis, instead of the state of denial and delusion that often exists.

Every family has to balance income and expenditure, and clergy families are no exception. However, the ordained member must always be on show and therefore there is no option to skimp in some areas. The family may have to take the brunt – possibly by eating cheaper meals or turning the thermostat down.

What about retirement?

In the previous chapter, there was mention of post-retirement housing. Anyone who lives in a tied house such as a vicarage is sitting on a time-bomb. When you retire, you will need somewhere to live. There are several options: you might be able to keep on the pre-ordination family home and rent it out until you need it, or can make use of its capital value to acquire a retirement home. If you have savings or legacies, they can be invested in property that can be used as a family bolt-hole or holiday home or, again, rented out until it or its capital value is needed for retirement.

This is all very well if you had property in the first place, or are able to finance its purchase. It is rather more serious if neither is the case, especially if you are living fully or partially off your wife's stipend. Should she need to retire early through ill-health, or should there be a divorce, separation or death before retirement, you could become homeless. The Church of England Pension Board and other bodies may be able to help in some circumstances, but it is essential that you take this seriously and address it sooner rather than later.

The bottom line

- Work out what your wife's ministry is going to cost, if necessary monitoring expenditure for a while; then review it with your wife and, if appropriate, the church.

- Negotiate with your wife how you will make decisions about what is spent on supporting her ministry and what is used for family expenditure, and how decisions are going to be made when there isn't enough for everything.

- Identify from the outset what is and is not paid for by the church, and make sure your wife gets it written into her working agreement.

- Find out what you can claim for and make sure you do. You may be able to donate it back again under Gift Aid.

- Find out what rebates and discounts are available to clergy. Most bookshops offer a discount, and there's even a specialist second-hand car company offering a service to clergy. Shop around.

- Plan for your retirement, starting yesterday!

16

Telephones, email and social networking

———◆◆◆———

Like doctors and dentists, we might all like to live in a world where we could restrict when people contact us, or even deter people from bothering us in the first place. But let's get back to the real world of a clergy household, where the telephone rings incessantly and the email inbox seems to fill up every time you turn your back.

The extent to which you need a coping strategy for telephones and emails depends on several variables:

- whether your wife is the incumbent or not, and whether she is in full-time or part-time ministry;

- whether you have a shared telephone number for church and family use or a separate one for your wife's exclusive use in her office;

- whether you have a single family email address that you share, or she has an exclusive one for church use;

- whether or not there is an answering machine, dedicated for her own use;

- whether you are the sort of people who are happy to let the answering machine do the work while you are dining;

- whether or not you use modern technology that allows you to allocate different ringing tones for different types of call;

- whether or not your wife has a private office in the home permitting church phone calls and emails to be ring-fenced, leaving the rest of the home in peace;

- whether there is a church office which in any case acts as a filter.

You may ask, isn't it all part of the job? You and the family have probably developed a good telephone manner, are efficient at message-taking, and are suitably inscrutable when required. Offering this service may not bother you, but that does not stop it being intrusive and time-consuming, especially if you would rather relax when you have finished your day's activities. And there are a number of specific issues to consider.

Confidentiality

It is essential to control access to confidential matters. People in distress or in crisis are liable to assume that speaking to a member of the clergy household is the same as talking to the clergy. You may unwittingly find yourself being told details of crises, emergencies and personal problems. Once you know, you cannot 'unknow' it, and you carry the burden of the knowledge ever after. You may be very good at it, but however willing you may be, it isn't your job. Should we expect our children and dependent elderly relatives to be equipped to respond with the discretion that we expect of ourselves?

You may consider yourself to be in joint ministry with your wife, but that confers no right to know. Even if you too are ordained, that may not necessarily entitle you to know about things said to your wife under the seal of confidentiality.

It is not possible to be prescriptive, and every family and church situation will be different, but some of the hazards described above can be avoided by taking the following simple steps.

- **Essential**: Install a separate line and answering machine for church calls: suggest that your wife discuss this extra cost with the church. Be aware, though, that your personal telephone number may become known, especially where family and friends are also church members.

- **Essential**: Create separate email addresses. Avoid email addresses which simply redirect church email messages (such as vicar@ email.co.uk) to a personal email address, since the moment your wife replies, her personal email address will be in the public domain anyway. Remember, once you have seen an email which was in fact confidential, you cannot 'unsee' it – you may wish you had remained in ignorance.

- Discuss with your wife ways of educating the congregation about appropriate times for calling your home, and the amount of information that it is appropriate to give to members of the household.

- Leave a message pad by all telephones in the home, and make sure that you have agreed where you will leave messages for your wife. Ensure that as a minimum you take the caller's name and number, the time of the call and the action required. Do not write down anything that you would not wish a third party to read. Cut the call short if the caller starts giving unnecessary or confidential information.

- Ensure that answering machines, whether for family or church use, have a 'mute' button and that nobody can hear messages being played back – they may be confidential.

Social networking

Many people now use the full range of electronic media to share their thoughts, to blog, to tweet and whatever else will have been invented by the time you read this. Sometimes these media are used deliberately by dioceses as an integral part of their communications strategy. Some clergy, including bishops, use this technology to express their opinions and observations on just about anything. Whether this is always wise is uncertain.

If it's all right for the clergy to do this, why shouldn't clergy husbands? In principle, there is no reason at all. However, what you may think of as a harmless comment may come across as being your wife's opinion when it isn't, showing her in a bad light, reflecting badly on the church, or appearing to be at odds with the faith that the church espouses. This is possibly no different from that thing we wish we hadn't said over coffee after the 10.30 service. The difference is that once it is out there, you have more or less lost control over who reads it.

If posting comments on social networks, think twice before hitting 'send'. Consider especially whether your perfectly valid personal opinions may come back to haunt you or your wife when seen in the context of her church position.

In conclusion, becoming your wife's unpaid personal assistant should be something you consciously decide to do. Some husbands will want to do this, but it isn't the case for everybody, and nobody is free of the potentially dangerous consequences of dealing with issues of confidentiality.

17

Quality of life issues

Children add a whole dimension of joy and blessing, but also repre-sent hard work, cost and organization. Many clergy husbands live in homes where the children, if any, have long since flown the nest. Grandchildren may play more of a part in their lives, with many of the same stresses and strains, though at least the children can be handed back at the end of the day! Even where children are not a consideration, however, management of days off, holidays and mealtimes all affect the equilibrium and the quality of life of the household.

The family

I am not well equipped to comment in this area as we don't have children, but, as they say, I know people who do. The whole life cycle from ante-natal, through birth and maternity, to nursery school, primary school, secondary school, and perhaps university, presents a range of issues that are part of every family's experience. These include childhood ailments, clothes, schools, exams, hormones and the rest of the package, and their impact on finances, use of time and share of duties. In so far as it affects every family with children, it affects clergy families.

How do you make sure that your sons and daughters can be normal children, when the outside world may expect them to be the embodi-ment of best behaviour, perfect attendance at Sunday school and full marks in school Religious Education tests? They may wonder why they can't play football with their mates on Sunday mornings, and why you think it inappropriate for them to watch something on television that all their friends are watching. Also, if you are the breadwinner and your wife is also working full time, how do you share the duties? Here are some suggestions:

- Explore the options for holding church meetings elsewhere, giving the children greater freedom to grow up in a home that has a semblance of normality.

- Have diary sessions to make sure that, like all other working couples, you manage some quality time with the children.

- Build into your financial calculations the additional commitments of having a family.

- Be open about any resentment you may feel about doing a second shift as nanny, housekeeper and laundry maid because your wife has so many evening and weekend commitments.

All of this makes it sound as if having a family is work, work, work, with no blessings. Of course the opposite is true in most cases, and it is a question of how to balance the overhead of having a family with reaping the blessings. One child of the vicarage observed:

> My family works around my mother's job. Of course it has had its effects on our family life but we have handled it well and I feel I have had a rich and full life so far as a result of my parents' actions, including my mother's career choice.

Days off and holidays

Just as sleep restores the body and repairs the strains and tensions of everyday living, so quality time together is essential for the individual and collective health of the whole family. That means that all clergy days off should be taken. They should not be thought of as discretionary. Of course things can crop up which require attention, but many clergy are their own worst enemies, accepting avoidable engagements on their days off, or getting ahead with the sermon or holding a meeting anyway.

The annual holiday entitlement should similarly be taken in full. Failure to do so damages the individual and the family, and, to be brutal, can suggest personal insecurity or a mistrust of those left behind to 'mind the shop'. In your wife's case, the need for recovery time from the emotions and pressures of ministry is critical. If she ignores this, it may affect her health and effectiveness, and the family may suffer by losing precious opportunities for time together. At a practical level it may stifle opportunities for others in the church to develop and pick up responsibility. To be fair, many clergy and their support networks in dioceses and deaneries have a very balanced view on this, but if you sense that your wife is for whatever reasons depriving herself of her entitlement, you have the right or even the duty to:

- encourage her to challenge deviations from planned days off and not let them be unilaterally decided, whether by her or the church;

- defend your right as a husband to quality time with your wife, and for the children to have quality time with their mother;

- protect your wife from herself.

Mealtimes

Let's keep this brief before we get interrupted!

- *Mealtimes mean you are available.* People know your wife has to eat, so they choose mealtimes to interrupt because they know she'll be in. Consider leaving the answering machine on and the front door unopened. Sounds easy? It isn't!

- *Weekend mealtimes are unpredictable.* At weekends, mealtimes may be totally irregular, because so many of your wife's working activities happen then, whether it's weddings on Saturdays or successions of services on Sunday.

- *Entertaining is a real challenge.* Entertaining at weekends may be impractical for your wife, but it will be equally hard for you and your guests during the week. It's worth the effort to find a way round this in order to protect important friendships and to keep in touch with the family.

In conclusion

As a clergy husband, you may find yourself impacted particularly hard by the fact that home, far from being an oasis of calm at the end of the working day, is an office, a meeting place, a telephone exchange and a nursery, and that you can't be certain that time off will be respected. Sometimes you must accept that you will have to come second, but given your wife's preoccupation with church matters, it may fall to you to defend the household's quality of life.

Lifestyle issues: key points

House or home?

Work out what you can do to make your house into a home, in such a way that the family can exist as naturally as possible, while enabling your wife to carry out her duties. Where there are compromises to be made, address them up front.

Don't be tyrannized by telephones and emails. Make the best use of technology to balance the needs of the family and the church.

Money matters

Understand the full range of expenditure that you will need to manage, understanding especially the implications of day-to-day costs and training. Support and encourage your wife as she negotiates these things with the church.

And so does time off

A life of service in the Church can often conflict with regular hours and time off. Do all you can to maintain a balance and encourage your wife to protect herself.

Retirement planning

Start now!

Part 4

IF THINGS GO WRONG

This section is optimistically titled '*If* things go wrong'. In reality, it is probable that at one stage or another, you and your wife will indeed find yourselves in some sort of difficulty. The aim of this part of the book is to shine a light on various areas of vulnerability so that you may see the potential risks and stop or change direction when the signals are still a pale shade of amber, long before the light shines red for danger. It can be used in several ways, and is intended for all readers, not just clergy husbands.

When I told someone I was including this section, they predicted that it would become the most thumbed part of the whole book. If that is you, I hope that you won't be disappointed when I say that I don't offer any answers or formulae. I am neither a qualified marriage counsellor nor a sex therapist; neither am I a theologian or an expert on church law. What follows, therefore, are thoughts on how clergy husbands may be affected by the same problems that affect all other marriages.

IMPORTANT

If you feel you are in the middle of something that has already gone wrong or is on the verge of doing so, please don't be alone but get help.

Most dioceses have someone who can assist in confidence, and if you want someone who comes without the baggage of the institution, there are many secular organizations and individuals with specialist skills and accreditations who can stand side by side with you. The internet can help you to contact such people without going through intermediaries you might feel could be embarrassing or prejudicial to your situation. But just as I would divert to an appropriate professional anyone sharing a confidence that I couldn't cope with or handle, I would stress that what follows is a starting point, no more.

This part of the book builds on the understanding we have now developed:

- Your wife's complex and extended journey from exploration of her vocation to the early stages of her ministry, and the impact on your marriage.

- The influence of personality and self-awareness, and the very personal set of beliefs, assumptions and principles that underlie your understanding of what it is to be a clergy husband.

- The impact of day-to-day factors that affect how and where you live, how you spend your time, where the money comes from and similar practical issues.

When these three work well, whether instinctively and intuitively or through a process of thought, preparation and negotiation, it is to be hoped that the clergy husband and his ordained wife and family may enjoy a successful and joyful life, largely free of major difficulties.

Why clergy marriages are different

Clergy couples are just that: couples, with the same difficulties, challenges and temptations as the rest of the population . . . and the same opportunities to succeed and share times of ecstatic happiness.

But clergy marriages are at particular risk. The world, the media, and even – or perhaps especially – congregations, place clergy families on precipitous pedestals, applying standards which would horrify them if applied to themselves. Then, if a member of the family falls from one of those pedestals, or slips perilously close to the edge, it may give rise to a disproportionate frenzy of self-righteous piety and prurience. Is it any wonder that people repress their feelings and their real selves, go into a state of denial, lose their faith, and suffer from mental or physical illness?

Cause and effect

It is natural to treat a difficulty, say a bout of stress, as if it were an isolated problem. In my professional life as a process improvement consultant, I help organizations to get to the heart of a problem and address the root causes. Very often, the problem that is presented is actually a symptom of something more serious, or the symptom is actually the cause of a more fundamental problem. Problems rarely exist in isolation, but usually reflect underlying issues. Try to be aware of the difference between cause and effect and be open to the fact that something relatively trivial may be concealing something far more serious.

Don't be alone

When things turn sour, it is a short journey to feeling completely isolated in shame, guilt and bewildered helplessness. You may feel that nobody could possibly have the same problems, have gone as wrong, be as unforgivable, or be as completely outside the redeeming love of God as you are. The sad thing is that with the right help and caught early enough, many of these things could be turned round relatively easily. That may sound daunting, but any counsellor or therapist will tell you that they ceased to be surprised by anything they heard very soon after they started in practice. As you read through the topics raised here, especially any that seem a little too close to home, make a note of them on a separate sheet of paper and use them to help you to see the risks early enough to stop that situation getting worse, preferably with a trusted friend, or an appropriate professional if that is what is needed. Don't be alone!

Don't pass by on the other side

People can be especially good at hiding problems, so the rest of us can hardly be blamed for not seeing the signs. Think of people's well-documented ability to conceal drink problems. Even when we do see the signs, we often prefer to collude and pretend nothing is wrong. Whoever you are, it is your business, if only out of love for your fellow creature, but especially when that creature is in service to you at one remove.

The pressures of being 'professional Christians' can turn the screw almost unbearably tight. This applies almost as much to a clergy husband as to his ordained wife. It can be little short of a disaster if we could have helped but actually did nothing. Genuine or feigned hand-wringing after the event is too little, too late. That's easy to say, for even if you do see the signs, you have to act with tact and delicacy. But that doesn't absolve you of responsibility.

Use this section to give yourself a feel for what to look for, how you could provide the right support, especially reminding yourself that the clergy husband in your midst is not a nameless irrelevance but potentially a critical lever to the success of his wife's ministry . . . and that he is a person in his own right.

Management matters

Who picks up the pieces, gets everything sorted out and keeps the press at bay? Someone in the hierarchy, the rural dean, the archdeacon or the bishop, possibly all of them, may participate in driving towards a successful resolution, or perhaps the 'least worst' outcome. If it is earlier in the journey, the DDO or perhaps the principal of a theological college may get involved. As in other fields, the buck stops with the management: if the Church requires or assumes the involvement of clergy husbands, whether directly or indirectly, in the ministry of female clergy, then the impact on those husbands needs to be taken into account. This section may therefore help you as a 'manager' to see the signs far sooner, thereby ensuring that things don't escalate, or that if they do, you are ready for them. More to the point, it may open your eyes to an aspect of your oversight that might previously have seemed irrelevant. Call it pastoral care or due diligence: the choice is yours.

18

Sex, adultery and addiction

—————◆•◆•◆—————

We were told via the archdeacon (I think), it doesn't matter
what you get up to in the bedroom – just don't get pregnant.
Bless!

Few things raise the temperature more quickly than the interplay
between the nobility of our spiritual calling and the earthiness of
our animal instincts. They are God-made, apparently intertwined,
and capable both of wondrous creativity and of destructiveness on
a major scale. In the face of the pressures and expectations that
the world places on clergy households, can we be surprised that the
destructive force of dysfunctional or misused sexuality, however
subtle and subliminal the signals, terrifies us into denial, collusion
and hypocrisy? Then, when it is too late to turn back the tide, the
dam bursts and all stability, certainty and peace are swept away in
a torrent of ruination. This is delicate ground, and it's no wonder
the media are so obsessed. The key questions here are: when does
sex become a problem? When does adultery start? When does an
absorbing interest become an addiction or an obsession?

Cause or effect?

When it becomes known that the clergy husband or the ordained
wife has become embroiled in inappropriate sexual activities, has
had an affair, or is having treatment for an addiction, it may seem
to those watching that this is the moment when that person's
world imploded into chaos and despair. My contention is that this
is merely the visible effect, the symptom of underlying chaos and
despair. It may all have started very subtly, almost imperceptibly:
a lingering glance, an ambiguous hug, a second bottle of wine at the
end of a trying week. There are clearly all sorts of triggers, many of
them quite innocent.

The slippery slope

The beginning of the slippery slope can, therefore, be imperceptible and the trigger for deterioration quite innocent, so much so that the idea that something might eventually cause damage is often counterintuitive. Here I will give an example, in this case exploring how becoming absorbed in something worthwhile may turn into obsession. For some years, on top of a busy job that took me away from home regularly, I was the conductor of an amateur choir that gave regular charity concerts. This involved a huge amount of work in my spare time, and the Tuesday night rehearsals were almost the easy bit. In parallel, I became involved in the leadership of the Cursillo movement in Scotland. The first was involved in making music while raising funds for good causes; the second with encouraging personal spirituality. What could be more innocent?

In fact my determination to get the job done meant that instead of devoting well-organized, compartmentalized time to these activities, I was apparently spending endless hours in my home office on the telephone or on my computer, steadily building a barrier between myself and my wife. It did not create long-lasting issues because she was firm enough and brave enough to confront me with the fact that I was beginning to treat her as incidental to our married life. Obsessive? I think so. Incipient addiction? I think you could say so.

Let's turn this round. Some clergy husbands feel isolated and lonely. They particularly bemoan the long hours that their wives work. I would argue that there can come a point where zeal for the kingdom and devotion to duty run the risk of tipping over into obsessive workaholism. You may disagree, but there are times, for instance, when the clergy do things that the laity could be doing, or when things are made over-complicated, to the point that the clergy may sometimes come across almost as 'professionally busy'. This lack of balance is potentially damaging to the ministry, health and marriage of the person concerned, with direct knock-on effects for the clergy husband and the family. It is immensely easy for their good will to be taken for granted by the clergy and by the wider Church, while the congregation generally remain oblivious.

In the meantime, loneliness or a sense of abandonment are likely to leave a void that may be filled in all sorts of ways, including a wide range of sexual and relational behaviours that we don't need to list here, but from which nothing is excluded.

Clergy husbands are also men

Hands up every clergy husband, in fact every man reading this book, who has never found his eye caught by an attractive woman, or for that matter, a hunk of a man. Yes, that means you. Never? Really?

The legal definition of adultery is sexual intercourse that takes place voluntarily between a married person and a person of the opposite sex, where the other person is not their spouse, while the marriage is still in existence. Let's pause to consider the contrast between this legal definition and the following Bible quotation: 'But I say unto you, that whosoever looketh on a woman to lust after her hath committed adultery with her already in his heart' (Matt. 5.28).

While the Gospel verse exaggerates for effect, it nevertheless makes a point that is especially relevant here: it is not the temptation that is the problem, but what you do about it. I remember being at a service many years ago at which a bishop – most definitely no names, no pack drill! – mentioned that he had been at the gym that morning and had enjoyed looking at all the women on the exercise equipment. Are you shocked? Appalled? Disbelieving? I can't remember why he said it, but if it was a confession of nothing else, it was of his masculinity, as God made him. His wife was there and enjoyed it as much as the rest of us.

Where, then, is the difference between admiration and lustful ogling? Just go back to my question and ask yourself again. And if you don't like your answer and would rather that I hadn't pressed you, do remember that God's redeeming love is capable of absolving you of the sin of letting your testosterone assert itself; it's more likely that it is you who is having trouble forgiving yourself.

Ambiguity

I suspect that highly charged church events can actually provide some of the most dangerous ground for physical temptation, those occasions when spiritual and emotional reactions collide, overlap and crunch against each other. In fact we may not know which is which, until we suddenly realize that a very proper and holy A-frame hug has become an all-out clinch.

In one case two friends were intensely involved in a highly charged residential church event and late one night found themselves on the brink of disaster. They saw the signs and walked away from the situation, which is just as well. Both were married to other people, and one was a clergyman.

So the slippery slope may start with something almost unnoticed at the time, possibly the intimacy resulting from working closely together on a project, however worthwhile. It is also the case that what is perfectly manageable for one person may be dangerous for another.

The acid test

If you have ever been in a situation like those alluded to above, here are two key questions:

- Would you be happy for your family to know about it?

- Would you be happy for your friends to read about it in the papers?

If the answer to either is 'Er, no!' then there's probably something wrong with it. It may not have been adultery according to the letter of the law, but are you going to tell your wife that you went for a drink with another woman and things turned a bit raunchy, or announce to your friends that you found an 'interesting' internet site?

Whether it is your behaviour or your wife's, the emotional and practical consequences could be catastrophic. If your wife has to leave her job, for instance, you could both end up homeless and in some cases without a source of income. Problems identified and confronted when they are still ambiguous are probably like cancers: caught early, they are more likely to be resolved.

Collusion and denial

Whether it is a question of inappropriate sexual behaviour, all-out affairs or addictions, recognition of the early signs may take us in one of two directions. If we are honest and open and react in time, then we may be able to change direction. If not, it is likely that matters will simply deteriorate.

It is natural to bargain, collude or go into denial, in the meantime carrying on with whatever it is, forever hoping that it will go away or even praying that God will 'cure' it. It's a bit like toothache! When I had a loose filling recently, common sense told me that I needed help, in this case 30 minutes in the dentist's chair and a fat bill at the end of it. Would that some of the things we are talking about here could be resolved as easily. But whether it's a toothache, sexual shame, an incipient affair or an addiction, I'm sorry, but it won't go away and needs to be dealt with before it becomes the marital or spiritual equivalent of having all your teeth out.

How should the Church react?

Is it rational to expect the Church to be closer to these things? In the first place, inappropriate behaviour tends to be well hidden. Even where there are suspicions it may be better for the Church not to become officially aware. Once they do, they probably have to intervene, with every possibility of exacerbating the mess, when it might have resolved itself if left alone. Sometimes, the best action may indeed be to turn a blind eye. Call it pragmatism or hypocrisy: it depends on your point of view.

COPING STRATEGIES

- See the signs, be honest with yourself and forgive yourself.

- If you can, walk away from any situation, practice or habit that could have destructive consequences for you or your family.

- If you observe such a situation in your spouse, or a friend or a colleague, don't pretend it isn't there, but find a way of bringing it out into the open.

- Find someone to talk to about it and don't be alone. It is no accident that the twelve-stage programmes for alcohol and other addictions are so successful, based as they are on openness, honesty and acceptance.

- And it needs to be said again . . . forgive yourself!

19

Career crises

The situation where both partners in a marriage go out to work is so common that it would be tempting to suggest that it doesn't merit any focus here at all. Unfortunately, however, there are characteristics of a clergy marriage that mean we must linger here a while. There are three scenarios to consider.

The ordained wife wishes to change role

Your wife feels called to move on to another parish that may be some distance from the current one. She may indeed be encouraged to do so. If you are in a career of your own, how will this move affect you and the family? It may require you to make a sacrifice of your own. The underlying tension may be more acute if your wife, like an increasingly large proportion of female clergy, is self-supporting and you are the breadwinner. Like 'ordinary' couples, you are both faced with a choice between two careers, but unlike those other couples, income is not necessarily the determining factor.

If you share your wife's sense of vocation and have committed to travel the journey with her, supporting her in every way, then this may not represent a serious hardship. What, though, if you are fulfilled in your own right and enjoy your own career? Do you feel angry? Undervalued? Marginalized? Confused? Emasculated even? Is it a consideration that you might have discussed when your wife's vocation was being explored? Perhaps, but the reality is that at the time, the idea of actually getting accepted for ministry was probably enough to think of without trying to second-guess the future.

Consider also the family. If the children are happily settled at school and have a network of friends and activities, any upheaval is likely to be hard for them. Even if your wife is in full-time stipendiary ministry which is the family's only source of income, it does not make the decision any easier. Unlike most changes involving promotion, it won't come with a pay rise, and relocation costs are unlikely to be covered in part or in full.

Oddly enough, the fact that your wife may feel 'called' to make this move, and that others, through a process of discernment, agree that the move is 'of God', doesn't necessarily make it any easier for you or for the children. It just makes it harder to seem anything other than churlish – and even unholy – if you raise any objections.

The clergy husband wishes to change job

You are offered a promotion or are required to relocate, meaning extensive travel away from home or the need to move house, even though your ordained wife is settled in her ministry and does not feel called to move.

This is hard. In many cases, you will have been married for some years before your wife entered the ministry. She will have contributed to household income from a secular job, and you will have been on your own career path. Unless you feel called to sacrifice your career and a large chunk of household income to support your wife in her calling, you are now faced with a major decision. In contrast to the previous scenario, your change may be accompanied by a pay rise, and any relocation costs will possibly be paid by the employer. On top of this, it is hugely flattering to be offered a promotion of this sort. Why wouldn't you feel justified in pursuing it? There is again the potential for a sort of moral blackmail: the fact your wife is either on a basic stipend or earning nothing at all should apparently be ignored because her calling is the 'more noble' one.

You may be angry and your pride may be hurt. She may feel rejected and undervalued. Perhaps this scenario, too, might have been anticipated, but it will have seemed a remote possibility at the time your wife went into the ministry. And, in any case, you might as easily have been made redundant.

Your job is made redundant

This is an especially complex situation, because so many areas of the family's equilibrium will be upset. At least in the first two scenarios, there is a sense that it is a nice problem to have. In this case, though, there can be a whole range of reactions. First, you may feel rejected as a person and may feel useless. After all, despite everything that outplacement agencies say, it may indeed have been the job that was made redundant, but you are the one who is out of work.

On top of these bruises to your self-esteem, the financial realities have to be faced. There will be practical consequences, sacrifices to be made; it could even reach the point where your wife is faced with hard decisions about her ability to continue in her particular ministry. Even if that drastic choice doesn't have to be made, you will now be looking for work, spending most of your time in a house from which your wife is exercising her ministry. You may be in the way, and it may become visible to you both, with short tempers and high emotions the result.

At a time of recession, redundancy is a common problem in many families, and clergy families cannot expect to be immune. Your redundancy, and everything that goes with it, may well affect your ordained wife's ability to present a composed front to the congregation and to individuals who seek her counsel. It is, in short, a time of family crisis, not just yours. I've been through redundancy three times, and although I am certain that I have come out of it a better person, I know that I experienced all those doubts, fears and emotional reactions; and although my wife was fully supportive throughout the process, the uncertainty affected her too, and in each case we were greatly relieved when the next step became clear.

Be aware, though, that the next step may require you to consider a job that involves a house move simply in order to get any job offer at all.

In summary

- It may seem counterintuitive to see a promotional job offer as the cause of crisis and confrontation, but it can be.

- Don't underestimate the power of money, or the potential lack of it, to destabilize your life and your relationship, even though you are a clergy family that 'ought' not to worry about such worldly things. Rubbish! Financial issues are one of the principal causes of marital strife, and you are not immune.

- Any loving relationship faces times when one partner or the other has to make sacrifices or face misfortunes. Clergy couples, especially those where both partners have a strong faith, may have a very slight edge over others, because they can bring God into the equation, but it is still hard.

You can't make contingency plans for everything that may affect careers, income streams and new lines of ministry, although communication, occasional reviews or reappraisals and, if it works for you, prayer, may mitigate to an extent. But some specific things you can do include:

- Encourage your wife to discuss her ministerial path well ahead, involving her training incumbent, her spiritual director or her peer group. Even clergy are frequently on fixed-term contracts, and it is good practice to be thinking of the next step sooner rather than later.

- Help to engineer your future career path by taking every opportunity that is offered to develop yourself, making full use of annual appraisals, and broadening your portfolio of experience. This can make it easier for you to apply for roles or promotions that work for you and your family. It may just help to make you the person they decide to hang on to at a time of job cuts.

At a time when wholesale redundancies are being made and entire business operations shut down, there is nothing that can be done to prevent or even predict redundancy. Our fate is generally out of our hands. This is a time for solidarity, application and friendships.

20

Loss of faith

———————

Loss of faith is something that can happen to anyone, and many books have been written about the signs, the possible causes, and suggested ways out of the misery. Here we are concerned with what happens when your wife has lost her faith, whether temporarily or, it may seem, permanently, or when you as the clergy husband lose yours – always assuming you were a person of faith before.

> **IMPORTANT**
> Don't wait until this problem arises, but read about this affliction when everything appears to be plain sailing, so you can understand any contributory factors and recognize some of the signs.

Your wife's loss of faith

Faith is a prerequisite of your wife's work. Without it, she would certainly not have been selected for training, ordination and a life of ministry. Her ability to speak with conviction and to lead others is dependent on her personal faith. Whereas many jobs are vocation-driven, there are few where the core is something so intangible, certainly indispensible, and yet sometimes ephemeral. Now, suddenly, as if someone had turned off the light, it seems to have gone, and her ability to do her job – indeed, its very meaning – appears to be without foundation. There seems to be no logic to it: some of the greatest theologians have had to endure what is sometimes described as the 'long night of the soul', something like a polar winter in which the sun never shines.

The impact of such an experience on your wife may be a mix of feelings of inadequacy, impotence, fear, anguish, guilt and failure. Whereas anyone else going through a similar problem might find solace in sharing the problem with others, ordained clergy are naturally reticent about announcing that their faith has vanished. At the very time when the support and prayers of a loving congregation would probably do most good, it may feel as if there is an imperative that nobody must know, even you. The personal impact of it has to come out somehow, whether in illness, breakdown, marital strife or some other downward spiral, and this is where your wife's loss of faith is likely to affect you. You may sense that something is not quite right, but you may not know what. For clergy, this is probably the ultimate career crisis.

Things that you can do

- Listen to the misery and pain without comment, but with love and acceptance, especially if you are someone of faith yourself.

- If an 'ought and should' theology is part of your own baggage, your first reaction may be to judge. This is hardly likely to help! Don't: it could be you next, however outlandish this may seem, and we are coming to that anyway.

- Encourage your wife to talk to the right people, her special friends or her spiritual director. If it seems appropriate, encourage her to discuss the matter with the rest of the clergy team. If she cannot do this, then that is a sign of a dysfunctional relationship that also needs attention.

- If you can, pray for her and with her.

Your own loss of faith

To lose your own faith is terrifying. You may have a strong sense of vocation, perhaps expressed in up-front ministry, whether or not you are ordained. This, too, depends on a personal faith. Even if you do not have your own public ministry, it may be this faith that fuels your ability to support your wife in her own ministry.

I am very fortunate in my faith journey. Although the valleys have sometimes seemed bleak, there has always been the slightest glimmer of light, a reminder of the blinding sunlight to be found on the mountain top. Others have different stories, and there is nothing as black as the darkness that follows the extinguishing of even the dullest glow.

Although loss of faith may not affect your ability to do your day-to-day job in the same way that it affects your wife, it may have a very similar emotional impact. On top of this, you may also feel guilty that you are letting your wife down and, unless you are better than most men at recognizing and expressing emotions, you may instead bottle it up, or sublimate it in other behaviours, thereby laying problems upon problems.

You may want to discuss your loss of faith with someone, but feel helpless. Perhaps it seems to you that if you talk to someone in the clergy team, it might reverberate onto your wife and how she is perceived. This is another reflection of the difficulty of identifying who is your parish priest when you are a clergy husband.

Advice, however well intentioned, may seem fatuous and smug. The best I can offer is the need to trust your wife with your pain, and to have your own network of friends, preferably including people outside your parish, maybe people with whom you share your faith journey on a regular basis. If you have established a deep rapport based on empathy and confidentiality, then, when something like this happens, you will have a ready-made safety net. A spiritual director can also be there for you, walking alongside you on this painful journey. At the risk of sounding like a scratched record, don't be alone.

Some people keep a spiritual journal, and if this is established as part of your way of life when things are going well, then there can be a cathartic benefit from pouring out on to paper your questions, your rage and your bewilderment.

At the beginning of this chapter, I suggested that loss of faith can be like someone switching off the light. Perhaps, though, there are contributory factors that lead to loss of faith and it is worth understanding them. Will such knowledge stop it happening to you or your wife? I don't know. After all, if faith is a grace, received as an unconditional gift from God, how can we know the reason why that very gift appears to have been taken away?

21

Discord within the parish

—————•◦•—————

Jesus wept.   (John 11.35)

See how these Christians love one another.   (Tertullian, *c.* AD 200)

When I read about the things that people get worked up about, I sometimes wonder whether Jesus is indeed weeping or whether he is falling about laughing, because the issues that seem to exercise us can be so petty as to defy logical explanation. It is rarely the things themselves that matter but what they stand for. For some reason we – and I include myself in this – have a tendency to want progress and change anywhere but in the Church, or wherever else it is that we find our stability.

The idea of replacing an ancient pipe organ that doesn't actually work with a digital instrument that makes a better sound than the pipe organ ever did, raises huge emotions, few of them related to musical expertise. Extend this to the flowers, the coffee rotas, which canticles are sung, whether the right candles are lit, something in the parish magazine, or the fact that the vicar visited Chloe but didn't visit Margaret. There will almost certainly be something similar that resonates for you and it is against this backdrop that day-to-day parish life can rapidly disintegrate into discord, sometimes played out in the local press, or even in national newspapers if the story seems sufficiently salacious. That such problems should arise in an organization which proclaims a gospel of love is especially tragic, and the worst possible picture to paint for the outside world.

For the clergy, these situations can be intensely painful. Hurtful comments and accusations may be levelled at them not because they are relevant or true, but because the clergy are a convenient target for people's hurt and anger. The discussion of boundaries in Chapter 11 is relevant here because your ordained wife may not be able to talk about a matter of this kind at all, at least in the early stages. Then, when you do eventually hear about it, it will generally be inappropriate for you to intervene.

Three types of discord are worth exploring.

Your wife's discord with clergy colleagues

This may involve a clash of personalities, failure to listen to one another, prejudice, exploitation of power and seniority, an absence of respect for family life and time off, or – perhaps the most significant given the environment – a lack of commitment to quality prayer time together. Whether the outward symptoms are the causes or simply the effects of a deeper malaise, it can be that pressure builds because of collusion to ignore the obvious, so that a relatively trivial incident suddenly ignites an inferno.

Opposition to female ordination and difficulties with the wider hierarchy are dealt with in Chapter 22, but it is not always possible to compartmentalize different issues, and there will often be a relationship between one and another.

As a clergy husband you may again be aware of nothing specific, only an atmosphere or a coolness. Members of the congregation may say things that you have to listen to without comment. You may feel that you are hearing only one side of the argument, when it is only loyalty to your wife that stops you taking a reasoned or conciliatory approach. It happens at some times in most parishes, and indeed in religious communities: ask the nuns in a convent whether they do indeed spend their entire lives gliding around in a state of sisterly love!

The collateral damage from this sort of discord can be extreme, including blocks to career progression, physical or emotional stress, and times when your wife doubts her faith. These consequences should not be ignored, but that doesn't leave a lot for you to do as clergy husband, even though the effects may spill over into family life. There are a few things that you can consider:

- Be aware that a snapped reply, periods of silence or tears, or unaccountable anger may be related to something your wife is unable to talk about.

- Encourage your wife to keep lines of communication open with her colleagues.

- Remain neutral if your church involvement means working with them.

- Listen without judging.

- Try to preserve the normality of everyday life.

- Keep your counsel and don't talk about the matter externally, even if someone who is uninvolved asks a question or raises the subject first.

Discord in the parish that directly involves your wife

In a way this is easier to cope with, because it will be out on the bush telegraph before you can blink. It may be a question of opposition to something that your wife has decided to do, such as a radical alteration to service formats or a change to church layout; or the discord may result from maverick behaviour within the congregation or the wider community. Either way, she will be involved in conflict management for which she may not have received training, the assumption being that her pastoral skills and her intelligence are all that she needs. She may wish to talk about it with you, if only to ensure that you are dealing in facts, not rumours. Some of the people involved may be your friends and you may need to keep them at a distance for the time being.

People also have a habit of striking out wherever they can: they write to the local paper, the archdeacon or the bishop, generally without telling your wife first, so the first she knows about it is when there is a call from the diocesan office, or a reporter appears on the doorstep. This is degrading and discourteous. The story may be inaccurate or incomplete or, more likely, so one-sided as to represent a distortion of the facts. Unfortunately, it may be hard to reverse initial reactions or prevent inappropriate and precipitate interventions.

Where does this leave you as the clergy husband? Perhaps as a fascinated spectator, but more likely full of righteous indignation on your wife's behalf. It is entirely possible, however, despite your loyalty to her, that she may have been at fault, and then you may have the delicate task of leading her towards that realization. It's easy to talk about humility, but everybody has their pride and self-esteem.

Conflict between you and parishioners

If you happen to be a protagonist in one of the dramas we have been talking about, it goes without saying, of course, that you are completely in the right! If you have become embroiled in a situation and despite your best endeavours have been a cause of discord, however, it will spin off on to your ordained wife. Whether you like it or not, and whether or not it is true, it will be assumed that she agrees with your point of view and with any action that you have taken. She may become the target of people's hostility, with drastic consequences for her ministry in your church.

By now it may be too late to do anything about such a situation, but it illuminates our earlier discussion of friendships, boundaries and the extent to which you get involved in the life and work of your wife's church.

If you are reading this at a time of crisis, make sure you know how to contact your trusted (non-church) friends, and be aware of any tendency to climb on to a soapbox at the first opportunity. Resist the temptation to get your wife to take sides and use the PCC or other church structures to fight your corner. It isn't her job and asking this of her may simply create further discord, this time in your marriage.

Final thoughts on discord

- Disagreements of this sort are rarely just one person's fault. There are always two sides to the argument, whether based on facts, prejudices or feelings.

- As clergy husband, you may be caught in the middle, but you may equally be powerless to do much more than mop the fevered brow and make a cup of tea.

- Any experience of conflict resolution that you have may be useful, but should be used with care as you will be considered part of 'the management'.

22

Opposition to female ordination

How much pain and anger can be generated by those who are prejudiced against women's ministry, or want to force it into a pattern of their choosing – especially those who say that they fully support it.

This chapter is not a discussion of the rights and wrongs of female ordination, nor does it seek to establish a case for or against the appointment of female bishops. Depending on your point of view and your experience over the last decade and a half, the ordination of women may or may not still be an issue for you. In general, though, despite some arguments to the contrary, it is clear that emotions still run high in places, and for some at least the topic remains live:

I underestimated the deeply embedded chauvinism that still exists in the Anglican Church.

Frustration with the sexism that still dominates our church, which ranks with the racism and the homophobia.

There is a sense in which if it were simply a question of being 'for' or 'against' female ordination, we would all know where we stand. Some churches would have female clergy, and others would not. End of discussion. Simple: choose your church according to your point of view. In the same way, the process of choosing where your wife is to serve her title as a curate would be a lot simpler, with the 'anti' churches filtered out. To an extent that probably already happens, since she wouldn't be offered an interview in the first place where female ordination is not recognized.

It could be argued, though, that the whole question is rather more subtle. Ambiguities still exist in how we feel, think and act and, perhaps, especially in the language we use. I was very struck by the following printed on a church service sheet: 'Please feel free to contact any of our clergy team, Father Andrew, Revd Barbara, Revd Caroline and Father Donald'.

We have not yet developed a language that is truly gender-less. Indeed, some have argued that we should celebrate the gifts of the masculine and the feminine with language that differentiates them more clearly. There is, however, no universally accepted equivalent to the courtesy title of 'Father' for a priest. How is the female priest to be addressed? And is she truly seen by her male colleagues and by the congregation as of equal status? I would suggest that the very fact of differentiating between male and female clergy in this way, in a parish where in all other senses they seem to coexist happily, sends out one of two subtle messages, both of 'unfinished business': either to do with not having quite worked out how it all works, or to do with not having fully accepted female ordination in the first place.

My 2011 survey showed that many clergy husbands support wives who still experience opposition ranging from the subtle to the downright misogynistic, whether sustained by sincerely held beliefs, or based on good old-fashioned bigotry. As a clergy husband, you are liable to get the flak and to experience the emotional fallout. But your position gives you no authority or licence to intervene, however much you may want to get on your white charger and ride to your wife's defence. Indeed, she may resent the intervention. All she wanted, after all, was a listening ear and sympathy!

Continuing opposition to female ordination, however subliminally expressed, may become a source of pain, anxiety, fractured relationships, and dysfunctional ministry for your wife; and the associated emotions may spill over into your married life and the way you relate to the parish that your wife serves. As with everything else, early action is likely to be most effective; what follows are some suggestions.

For clergy husbands

- At the time of selecting a parish, especially for your wife's first curacy, become involved, even if you are not an active Christian believer. Take the temperature of the parish on female ordination, not just in what they say, but in what you see of the church. Compare notes with your wife, and make sure that the potential for problems to arise is addressed as part of the decision-making process.

- Similarly, if these issues arise once she is in post, listen to her; sympathize, give her a shoulder to weep on, make her a gin and tonic. Resist the temptation to intervene. It is her vocation, not yours, and she must decide the appropriate stance.

- The fact that you react to the situation means you have strong feelings about it. Have someone to discuss them with, preferably outside the parish.

For the congregation

- If you have an opinion on female ordination, make sure you can articulate it clearly and that you know when and how it is appropriate to express that opinion. If it stands up to scrutiny, hang on to it. If it does not, think it through again. Be brave!

23

The church hierarchy

———————·•·———————

While I was writing this book, I received an email from a clergy husband saying: 'You do need to be aware that if it comes out largely negative or even balanced it could cause trouble for both you and more particularly for your wife. It could easily affect whether she gets a job!'

While my intention was never to provide a soapbox for people to have a moan, or to generalize on the basis of very specific situations, neither does my intellectual integrity permit me to pretend that things haven't been said, and this is especially apposite in the case of clergy husbands, who are at only a single remove from the Church as an organization. There is a perception, for some at least, that the institution is not wholly to be trusted. The evidence for this is that some clergy husbands declined to take part in the survey, fearing that they might be identified, with unfortunate repercussions for them or their ordained wives, while others contributed only on condition that their names and locations should be concealed, for the same reasons.

My experience of the Church of England has been rather more benign: I smile at its eccentricities and at the way it sometimes goes about things. I do share with others some misgivings on the way the Church handles people, especially given its tight resources. In the research, respondents were asked to comment on any times of pain or disappointment that they had experienced. The following comments came from respondents who in all other respects were generally positive:

It's nearly six months since the ordination, and nobody has asked either of us how we are getting on. We obviously don't matter.

[I'm] raging at how the institutional Church can so often be a barrier to mission, ministry and growth.

Frustration and anger when the Church seems not to appreciate how much it needs and benefits from the ministry of women, and of non-stipendiary ministers, and of lay people. Some (but not all) in the hierarchy can be very arrogant and take this ministry for granted, or put little value on it.

I wish I had known how shambolic the Church was in its approach to employment issues.

Beware archdeacons trying to fill holes!! They are nice people, but their job is to fill vacancies, and sometimes they put that before the best interests of the person searching for a new post.

Having to live separately just as she was ordained because no housing had been arranged for us.

There is no one to check whether the priest is working himself/ herself into an early grave.

I tend to think the hierarchy give little thought to spouses, whether male or female. In all my time in this role I think I have only been to three or four events for clergy spouses, and some of those were pretty ad hoc. Of course there are wonderful exceptions, but the overall system is still set up for young male single curates and vicars.

Some parts of the hierarchy can be jolly vindictive!

The Church is one of the most dysfunctional organizations I have come across.

Whether or not these comments are truly representative is open to question. For many, life is joyful, with many achievements, blessings and successes to celebrate, and with minimal exposure to the institution of the Church. In these cases the husband, often a person of deep faith, offers a quasi-vocational support role that makes it possible for his wife to exercise her ministry. Indeed, some of these clergy husbands would be astonished to see this chapter here at all. But others clearly take a rather more jaundiced view, believing that there is an unquestioning assumption of their good will and acquiescence.

Even when things are not ideal, however, we have to accept that we won't change the Church in a hurry. It has taken centuries to reach its current state, and there are many who would not wish it to change at all. Nevertheless, here are some things to think about:

For clergy husbands

- Don't think you can change the Church. You can't, so don't waste energy thinking that you can!

- Leave your ordained wife to fight her own battles with the hierarchy. You are more likely to be resented if you intervene, and, seriously, it may have repercussions for both of you if handled inappropriately.

- Cut the Church some slack! It's a huge organization, under-resourced financially, trying to address major cultural shifts that threaten the stability of the institution. It's led by people who have many fine qualities, but who are not necessarily equipped with the skills and experience required to manage a large organization.

For female clergy

- Don't underestimate any feelings of injustice that your husband may have on your behalf, but gently dissuade him. If there is a fight worth fighting, then it's up to you to decide what to do, how and when.

For the wider Church

- How much attention do you give to part-time and/or self-supporting clergy, especially female clergy, compared to other clergy?

- How well do you know your clergy husbands? Do you know what work they do or how they contribute to church life?

- What procedures are in place to ensure that you meet the husbands of your female clergy within a reasonable time following ordination?

- What mechanisms exist to meet the particular needs and concerns of clergy husbands?

- What safeguards exist to protect the family life of your clergy, including insistence that they take quality time off together and don't work excessive hours?

If you don't think that any of this is your responsibility, ask yourself why not. If not yours, whose responsibility is it?

24

Illness and bereavement

———•·•·•———

It would be inappropriate to end this book without exploring the one area that is almost completely unavoidable and unpredictable. Illness and bereavement can arrive to torment us so cruelly and unexpectedly that one is sometimes left with the lingering question, however firm one's faith, however solid one's theological ground, of how a loving God could conceivably permit these things to happen. I don't know. But the fact is that illness and bereavement are part of the lot of all families.

> **IMPORTANT**
> All of the scenarios described below appear rather bleak. Be assured that many church organizations have mechanisms to help and you will be supported both in practical ways and by the prayers of people known and unknown. You are not alone, however much it may feel so.

Illness or bereavement in the clergy team

There can be serious repercussions for everyone when a member of the parish clergy team is affected by illness, accident or bereavement. Everyone will of course be saddened and wish to rally round, but all the usual tasks still need to be done. In a small team this generally means everyone working harder, usually at a time when everyone is preoccupied, saddened or feeling the deep loss of bereavement. As a clergy husband you may observe your full-time ordained wife working even harder (if that were possible!), or your part-time ordained wife working far longer hours than are in her working agreement.

You may find the rhythm of home life is disrupted even more than usual by unexpected events, involvement in things that normally happen elsewhere, or people seeking comfort and support. There may be increased reliance on you as the clergy husband to keep the household ticking over, taking on day-to-day tasks that your ordained wife normally does. And there may be tiredness, emotional reactions and frayed nerves all round, though equally a crisis can bring out the best in everyone.

This is a time for pulling together, of course, especially if what is happening is an extended period of illness, possibly terminal, with greater sadness still to come and possibly the extra tribulations of an interregnum to follow.

Your wife's illness

We are not talking here about a short bout of flu, but something longer lasting or which may need intensive treatment. How your wife's illness impacts on the church, and therefore on you as the clergy husband, will depend in part on whether she is in full-time or part-time ministry, and whether she is stipendiary or non-stipendiary. This is simply because these different styles of ministry may influence the range of tasks and responsibilities that she usually undertakes. The impact on the clergy husband will include being moved at the way everyone rallies round and wants to help, while juggling work and household duties, including increased involvement in child care and looking after dependent relatives.

If your wife is in stipendiary ministry, household income may be affected if she is only on full stipend for a limited period and the illness extends beyond the statutory period. This may be an added source of anxiety.

You may ultimately find yourself making career decisions so that you may be available to care for your wife. This too may have financial implications. And in the event that your wife is unable to resume work and needs to retire early on medical grounds, then there may be a housing issue if you are in a church-owned house.

The impact of an ordained wife's death while still in post

You are unlikely to be reading this book if such a sad event has just taken place, so these observations are offered on the basis of 'forewarned is forearmed'. Whether your wife's death is the result of illness or accident, you, your family and the wider church community will experience the full range of emotions that are experienced by all in similar situations. There are two practical issues to be taken into account:

- If she was in stipendiary ministry, then, like any other home where the wife was a source of family income, there will be some thinking and replanning to do with the passage of time.

- If you are living in a church-owned house, then, sadly, there will come a time when alternative arrangements will need to be made. Most church organizations will be very sympathetic and helpful in this area.

It also needs to be said that if you, too, have an active role in the church, whether or not ordained, you will need to lay down many of these tasks, at least in the short term. You may feel reluctant to do so, as getting on with things may feel like a way of getting to grips with life, but that might be unsettling for others, and may be putting off the business of grieving.

Your own illness

If you as the clergy husband are ill for an extended period, this may impact on your family, on your wife's ability to do her work, and also on family income if the illness extends beyond a certain period. This is something you need to discuss with your wife if you are well enough to do so. It will certainly be an issue if you have been shouldering much of the responsibility for managing the home so that she is free to get on with her work.

The effect of stress

In church life, people like your wife are frequently overstretched and work in isolation, often in the face of huge expectations and entrenched positions. The life they share with their families is often played out in conditions of financial hardship and less than ideal living conditions. It is no wonder that people become stressed. This is perhaps the most insidious sort of affliction, because it can be hard to recognize in the first place. And it can be difficult to distinguish between helpful stress, where adrenalin stimulates beneficial outcomes, and unhealthy stress that can result in longer-term illnesses, depression and mental illness, which can in turn lead to life-threatening conditions or even death. Just about any of the situations described in this book can result in stress, especially if not recognized or confronted early enough.

If you or your wife are reading this at a time of stress, then you need to get the right help now, not read a lecture on how to avoid stress! Otherwise, be aware that stress can be a real risk to your wife's life of ministry and to yours as a clergy husband. There are ways to mitigate this risk:

- Consider the earlier parts of this book on the original journey, what it is to be a clergy husband and practical lifestyle issues, and discuss with your wife whether there are things that you could do differently or more effectively.

- Take care of yourself. Protect time off and holidays, enjoy a good diet, fresh air and exercise, stimulate your mind with non-church things, and cosset your spiritual health. In short, take care of your body, mind and spirit.

Conclusion

Illness and bereavement are unpredictable: you cannot generally anticipate either what might happen or its emotional impact. There's little point in having pessimistic 'what if?' conversations about every conceivable thing that might afflict you and your family. Some things can only be experienced when they actually happen.

Remember, therefore, that you will not be alone. The people around you will provide support, will be there when you need them, and will leave you alone if that works better for you. While you suffer, however opaque the veil that seems to obscure God's love, and however violent the anger you feel towards the loving God who seems to have turned his back and forsaken you, others will be holding you up in prayer, lowering you through the roof on a pallet for God's healing touch.

If things go wrong: key points

Things within our control

I used to have a bookmark with the ribbon attached to a hole in the wrong place and printed 'pobody's nerfect'. How true! Whether it is the subjects you would prefer not to talk about, like sex, adultery and addiction, or your capacity to say the wrong thing, upset people or be obstinate, you are not immune from getting it wrong. Most of it, though, is at least to an extent within your control. What you do about it and how you react can help to minimize the damage to yourself and others.

- Be aware of your weak areas and wherever possible recognize the signs early. Walk away from the situation and get help before there is real damage.

- Forgive yourself! Guilt and misery may be natural reactions, especially for a clergy husband, but they don't make things any better. Why add stress?

Things that people do

The fact that we have explored the potential damage of discord within the parish, opposition to female ordination, and difficulties with the church hierarchy should not be taken as a suggestion that these are the experience of every clergy husband. Many people go through life without encountering any of them. In any case, some people are equipped to respond more phlegmatically than others to such issues, depending on their personalities. The key point here is that you generally cannot change people or organizations, however much you may disagree with them or find them difficult to work with. What you can do is:

- Decide which fights are worth fighting and ignore the rest.

- Choose your attitude and assume innocence. The same issues can be handled calmly and constructively, or stressfully and in an adversarial manner. You have a choice.

- There used to be an advertisement with the caption: 'We don't make a drama out of a crisis.' By distancing yourself from other people's emotions, you can help to defuse a difficult situation before it does indeed become a crisis.

Things that just happen

I have deliberately left this to the end, because any of the issues described in this book may lead directly or indirectly to the deterioration of your wellbeing or that of someone near to you. Their effects can be heartbreaking, especially if they seem to happen out of the blue. For illness, accident, bereavement, sudden loss of faith and redundancy, I can offer nothing but sincere sympathy and the following suggestions:

- Always be aware of the potential of anything to be stressful, and for that stress to manifest itself physically, mentally or spiritually.

- In the isolated world of a clergy husband, nurture your friendships and allow people to care for you if the need should arise.

- It is not for nothing that the Bible says that your body is a temple. Cherish it!

A final word

This book started with a glimpse of my life as a clergy husband. Any more would have been an intrusive distraction, because this is all about your story as a clergy husband, or his wife, associate or friend.

For many clergy husbands, life is satisfying, fulfilling and exciting. If you are one of these, I rejoice with you. This is not true for everyone, however, and in any case the two things we all have in common are our human frailty and the fact that bad things can happen to anyone.

I certainly don't want to deter you from enjoying life, but I do want to help you to form your own picture of who you are as a clergy husband, the sorts of experiences you may encounter, the things that may affect the quality of life and an awareness, though not, I hope, the experience of pitfalls along the way. If you remember nothing else from this book, therefore, try to keep in mind three recurring themes:

- know yourself;

- you have a choice;

- don't be alone.

Let the last word, therefore, be with Shakespeare:

> This above all – to thine own self be true,
> And it must follow, as the night the day,
> Thou canst not then be false to any man.
> (*Hamlet*, 1.3.78–80)

Resources

This book contains a number of ideas and suggestions, and I hope that whatever your reason for reading it, you will use it above all to stimulate thought and dialogue. Should you want to explore any of the themes in greater depth, I would suggest that the starting point will be your diocese or church, since they generally offer excellent support and resources to cover a wide variety of situations. But this section also lists some books, web sites and organizations that you may find helpful.

Personal spirituality

Alan Hargrave, *Living Well*, London: SPCK, 2010
Gerard W. Hughes, *God of Surprises*, London: Darton, Longman and Todd, 1985
Henri Nouwen, *The Return of the Prodigal Son*, Doubleday, 1992
John Pritchard, *How to Pray*, London: SPCK, 2011

Daily meditations:
www.cacradicalgrace.org/get-connected/emailsubscriptions

Anglican Cursillo:
www.anglicancursillo.co.uk

Male spirituality:
www.malespirituality.org/masculine_spirituality

Loss of faith

John Pritchard, *God Lost and Found*, London: SPCK, 2011

Pastoral care

Every diocese has a pastoral care advisor, although the title may be slightly different in your area. You could also read:

Kate Litchfield, *Tend My Flock*, Norwich: Canterbury Press, 2006

Clergy spouses

Johanna Fredrickson and William A. Smith, *How the Other Half Lives*, Cleveland, OH: Pilgrim Press, 2010
Sara Savage and Eolene Boyd-Macmillan, *The Human Face of Church*, London: SCM, 2007.

Jane Williams (ed.), *Marriage, Mitres and Being Myself*, London: SPCK, 2008.

Spiritual direction

Don't be put off by the title spiritual director: if you think in terms of a soul-mate or a companion, it will give you a better feel for the nature of this ministry. An internet search will give you a greater feel for what spiritual direction is, and your diocesan web site will probably have practical details about finding a spiritual director.

Pensions/retirement planning

www.churchofengland.org/clergy-office-holders/pensions-and-housing

Marriage problems

www.brokenrites.org
www.relate.org.uk

14306875R00072

Printed in Great Britain
by Amazon.co.uk, Ltd.,
Marston Gate.